GO SCIENCE!

Motivation Progression Success

Series editor:
Byron Dawson

BOOK 3

Berry Billingsley

David Lees

Dave Mason

Sally Morris

Helena Ward

Sian van der Welle

ANALYSE

SCIENTIST AT WORK

www.heinemann.co.uk

✓ Free online support
✓ Useful weblinks
✓ 24 hour online ordering

01865 888118

Heinemann

Contents

Key to focus on how science works symbols

 investigation

 analysing data

 science in the news

 science and the world around us

Contents

How to use this book

Welcome to *Go Science!* We believe that learning about science, what scientists do and how science works should be fun. So we've packed in lots of amazing photos and illustrations, foul facts and interesting facts, as well as different types of exciting pages including 'setting the scene', 'focus on how science works' and the 'best science lessons ever'.

Here are the main types of pages in *Go Science!*

These are the 'setting the scene' pages. They tell you what you are going to be learning about in the chapter.

Here are some questions to get your brain warmed up before you get into the main lessons.

Read about the illustration. If you have the **LiveText CD-ROM**, you will be able to click on 'hotspots' around the photo to discover more.

These photos and captions give you some clues about what is coming up in the chapter. If you have the **LiveText CD-ROM**, you will be able to click on these photos and find out more.

This is one of the main lessons. This box tells you what you will be learning about in the lesson.

Questions in the text make sure you have understood what you have just read. They are colour coded and the levels are in brackets, so you know what level you're working at.

Foul facts are about the 'yucky' parts of science.

The keyword box lists all the keywords in a lesson. If you have the **LiveText CD-ROM** you can click on the glossary word and a pop-up box will give you its definition.

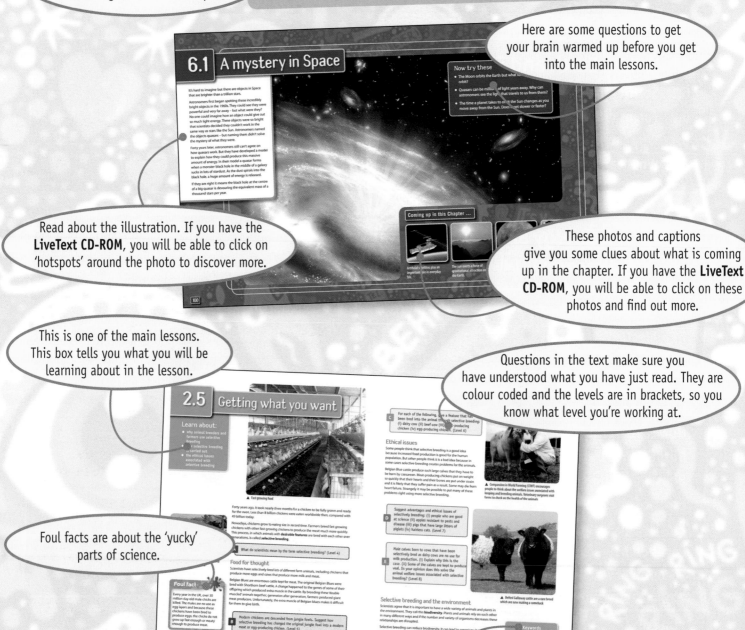

In this 'Focus on how science works' lesson you will look at some real scientific research.

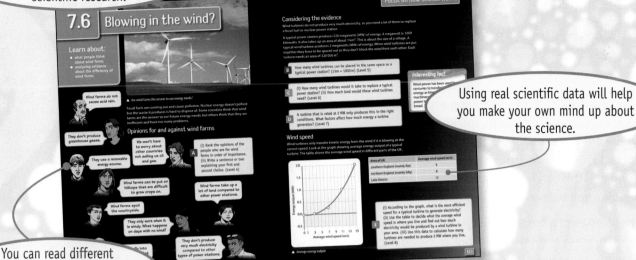

Using real scientific data will help you make your own mind up about the science.

You can read different people's views and make up your own mind.

We asked you what you liked most about science and many of you said it was the practicals, so we've included some 'best science lessons ever' in the book.

Here's a step-by-step guide to what you will be doing in the practical.

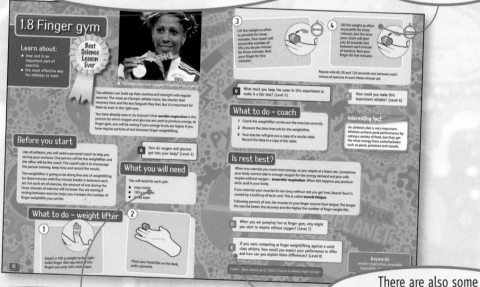

There are also some questions for you to answer.

Here's a list of what equipment you will need.

Key to question colours

 Level 4

 Level 5

 Level 6

 Level 7

Level 8

At the end of the book, there are spreads focusing on how science works, spreads that will help you revise and some sample practice questions.

On the **LiveText CD-ROM**, there are seven extension lessons that don't appear in this book. These help you practise your scientific skills.

A hearty lifestyle

Lifestyles are constantly changing and this is having an effect on people's health. You live in a society where it is common for people to work long hours, eat fast food and do little exercise. Obesity levels are rising and this can have serious consequences on people's general wellbeing and health.

The stresses of a modern lifestyle are also linked to an increase in drinking alcohol, smoking and drug taking. Many adults and teenagers use these drugs as a way to relax. These substances can have devastating effects on the human body.

As a living organism, you carry out the seven life processes. It is when these life processes are affected by your lifestyle that you may begin to experience health problems.

The United Kingdom has one of the highest rates of death from heart disease in the world. An unhealthy lifestyle puts you at greater risk from serious diseases and can lead to an early death. So, what can you do to keep your body healthy?

Now try these

- List the seven life processes.
- Why would eating fast food put you at greater risk of a heart attack?
- Compare and contrast the typical days of a healthy and unhealthy person.

Coming up in this Chapter ...

How can you train your body to run a marathon?

The gruesome facts about cigarettes

A good night out or a bad night for your body?

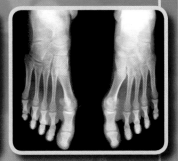
How science can help repair our bodies

1.2 Wow, you're fit!

Learn about:

- different types of fitness
- measuring fitness levels
- how to improve fitness

▶ How can Nick prepare his body to run 26.2 miles?

Nick is planning to run the next marathon. While training, he measures his **pulse rate** at rest and after exercising.

A Describe what happens to Nick's pulse rate after he does the different types of activity shown in the table. (Level 4)

Nick's pulse rate after different types of activity

Activity	Pulse rate (beats per minute)
resting	65
walking	71
jogging	115
sprinting	137

What is fitness?

Your **fitness** is how well your heart and lungs can deliver oxygen around your body. Your **pulse rate** is one way to assess how well your body can do this. While you exercise, your muscle cells need an increased supply of oxygen and glucose to produce energy. If you are fit, your body will deliver this oxygen easily and you will be able to continue exercising for longer. If you are unfit, your lungs will take in less oxygen from the air and your heart will struggle to pump enough oxygen-rich blood to your muscles.

B Why do the muscles of unfit people get tired more quickly than those of fitter people? (Level 5)

C Why is Nick's pulse rate so high after sprinting? (Level 6)

Only 20% of people get enough exercise to keep them healthy. If you want to get fitter you should try to do 1 hour of exercise a day.

After several weeks of training, Nick notices that his resting pulse rate gets slightly lower. His trainer tells him this change is because his heart is becoming more efficient at pumping blood around his body.

Different kinds of fitness

Although his training includes a lot of running, Nick also works out in the gym to help build up muscle strength. Muscle strength is another way of measuring fitness.

Different types of athletes have different types of **fitness**:

- Bodybuilders need to build up the size of their muscles, so lift weights.
- Sprinters need to be able to run extremely fast but for relatively short distances, so train by working on their speed and technique.
- Marathon runners need to be able to run for long periods, so train by doing a high level of exercise for a long period of time.

▲ Bodybuilders lift and pull heavy weights to increase their muscle mass

Training to be fit

Nick has to be careful about what he eats too. Different sports people need different diets and training.

Comparison of fitness training			
Fitness type	Calories per day	Major food group	Daily exercise
(weightlifter)	3800	protein	weight training 3 hours a day 6 days a week
(sprinter)	2900	protein	running and gym 5 hours a day 6 days a week
(runner)	2500	carbohydrate balanced diet	30 minutes moderate exercise 5 days a week

D Compare the three types of daily exercise shown in the table above. Which one do you think is the safest and why? (Level 7)

Going to extremes

Exercise is good for you, but it is possible to overdo it. When you exercise your body releases **endorphins** – these are **hormones**, chemicals that circulate in the blood. Endorphins make you feel good. Some people may become **addicted** to these hormones and the feeling it gives them. Extreme exercise can also be linked with eating disorders such as anorexia.

Extreme exercising can also damage your bones and joints causing **osteoarthritis** and fractures. Muscles are also at risk of damage, including tears and strains.

▲ Tearing a muscle can be extremely painful and can take months to heal

E Osteoarthritis is normally associated with old age. (i) Explain why over-exercising may bring this on early in life. (ii) Which types of exercise may lead to osteoarthritis? (Level 8)

Keywords
addicted, endorphins, fitness, hormone, osteoarthritis, pulse rate, sports psychologist

5

Learn about:

- how scientific understanding changes people's behaviour
- how smoking affects the life processes

▼ The mechanics of breathing

Breathing in

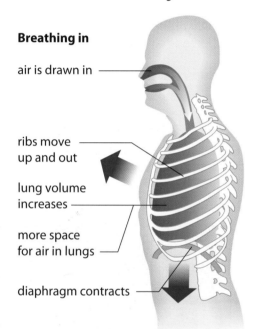

air is drawn in

ribs move up and out

lung volume increases

more space for air in lungs

diaphragm contracts

Breathing out

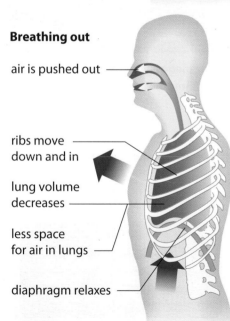

air is pushed out

ribs move down and in

lung volume decreases

less space for air in lungs

diaphragm relaxes

The Victorians used to think smoking was good for you and cleared the lungs. When you watch an old film you often see film stars smoking. They thought it would make them seem more glamorous. Cigarettes were shipped out to soldiers in the First and Second World Wars to boost morale. It was only when the scientific link between cigarettes and health problems was made that attitudes towards cigarettes began to change.

▲ In the 1950s doctors were paid to advertise cigarettes to make them appear healthy

Getting a lungful

Breathing is controlled by the muscles surrounding your lungs. Two sets of muscles are involved. The **diaphragm** is a muscular sheet beneath the lungs. There are also muscles between each rib. The muscles between each rib and in the diaphragm contract and relax, drawing air into and out of your lungs. This is called **ventilation**.

A Describe the process for breathing in. (Level 4)

To ventilate the lungs, air is drawn in through the nose and mouth and down the **trachea** or windpipe. The trachea is lined with **specialised cells**. These cells have adaptations that protect the lungs from microbes and dirt that we breathe in. The cells have small hairs called **cilia**. Movement of the cilia pushes the mucus and trapped particles back up the trachea. The mucus and trapped particles are either then swallowed or coughed up.

B Describe how ciliated cells keep the lungs healthy. (Level 5)

What cigarettes do

A chemical in cigarettes called tar destroys the cilia. Without the cilia, dirt, microbes and mucus build up and can pass into the lungs. This can cause damage and infections such as **bronchitis**. This is also why smokers often cough a lot.

▼ The effects of smoking on ciliated cells

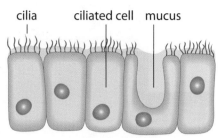

cilia   ciliated cell   mucus

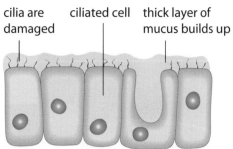

cilia are damaged   ciliated cell   thick layer of mucus builds up

Non-smoker with healthy ciliated cells and thin layer of mucus

The ciliated cells of a smoker, only a few cilia left, thick layer of mucus

C Smoking makes the lungs less stretchy. Explain how this contributes to heavy smokers becoming breathless and tiring easily. (Level 6)

What's in a cigarette?

Cigarettes contain lots of harmful chemicals. The table shows a small sample of them.

Chemicals in cigarettes	
Chemical	**Effect**
30+ different carcinogens	cancer
nicotine	addictive – makes it hard to stop increases blood pressure
tar	destroys cilia
carbon monoxide	lowers amount of oxygen blood can carry

Foul fact

If the nicotine from one cigarette was injected directly into your veins, you would be dead in seconds.

D Using the information from the table, which chemical would decrease the fitness level of a smoker and why? (Level 7)

Since smoking became common at the beginning of the twentieth century, a **positive correlation** between smoking and lung cancer has been identified by scientists. A positive correlation occurs when there is a definite link between a cause and effect. In 1912 there were only around 350 cases of lung cancer, now there are over 35 000 deaths a year.

A deadly habit

Smoking doesn't just affect the lungs. As well as causing cancer of the lungs, the chemicals in cigarettes cause many other types of cancer. Smokers are also more likely to get colds, gum disease, heart attacks, high blood pressure and have sleep problems. Smokers also age prematurely.

Passive smoking can be just as harmful. Smoke released into the environment by a smoker still contains all the harmful chemicals. Regular passive smoking increases your risk of getting lung and heart disease as well as developing cancer. Children of smokers are more likely to develop respiratory problems such as **asthma**.

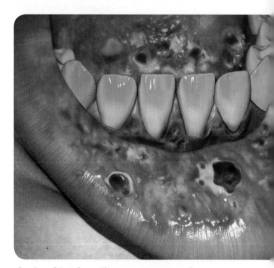

▲ Smoking heavily can cause mouth cancer

E In July 2007, a new law was introduced banning smoking in public places. What effect do you think this will have on the health of the nation and why? (Level 8)

Keywords
asthma, bronchitis, cilia, diaphragm, passive smoking, positive correlation, specialised cells, trachea, ventilation

The deal on drugs

Learn about:

- why some drugs are legal and some are illegal
- the problems of drug taking
- how science is used to inform the public

▲ Which of these people are taking drugs? The answer is: all three

A **drug** is a chemical that affects the way your body works. There are three different groups of drugs: **medical drugs**, **legal drugs** and **illegal drugs**.

The hard facts

Drug groups			
Type of drug	**What they are**	**Examples**	**Where they are available**
medical drugs	Substances that are used to prevent, cure or treat a disease or illness. They are tested before being used on patients and their use is closely controlled.	painkillers and antibiotics	You can either buy these drugs from a pharmacy or see your doctor for a prescription.
legal drugs	Substances that act on the brain and make you feel more alert, relaxed or happy.	alcohol, caffeine, nicotine and solvents	Alcohol, caffeine, nicotine and solvents are available in shops. You have to be a certain age to buy alcohol, nicotine and solvents.
illegal drugs	Substances that governments have decided are potentially harmful so have made it against the law to possess them. These drugs can cause long-term damage to your body and are potentially fatal.	cannabis, ecstasy, heroin and speed (amphetamines)	Illegally sold by drug dealers.

A Which types of drug are the following: (i) cannabis (ii) alcohol (iii) paracetamol? (Level 4)

10,000 BC	4,000 BC	1450 AD	1675 AD	1850 AD	1906 AD	1975 AD	1978 AD	2004 AD
Crops of tobacco, coffee and cannabis grown	Beer making in Egypt	Coca leaves (where cocaine comes from) used by Incas	Coffee houses in England	Cocktails invented in New York	Coca leaves removed from Coca Cola formula	Coffee shops in Amsterdam start selling cannabis	Ecstasy hits the streets	Cannabis reclassified from Class B to Class C

▲ The history of drug taking

B   Take a look at the history of drug-taking timeline. What types of drugs were used in 10 000 BC? (Level 5)

The problems

All drugs have the potential to damage the body. If you take medical drugs incorrectly, particularly if they are prescribed for someone else, they may damage your body. Some drugs can also cause addiction. You are addicted when you develop a physical and mental dependency on it. This means that when you stop taking these drugs you may suffer from **withdrawal symptoms**. These make you feel ill.

Are certain people more likely to become addicted to drugs than others? Some scientists think that some people have addictive personalities, and it is these people who are more likely to become dependent on any type of drug.

Scientists have shown that alcohol, caffeine, nicotine and some medical drugs all affect a woman's ability to get pregnant. They have also proved that taking some types of drug while pregnant can be harmful. Any substance that is in the mother's bloodstream will be passed to her baby. While a baby is developing in the uterus, even a small amount of the drug could be harmful. Some chemicals in drugs, such as cigarettes or steroids, can also affect how a baby grows.

C   What effect does alcohol have on your body that makes it dangerous to drive after you have been drinking? (Level 6)

D   (i) Describe in detail, with the aid of a flowchart, how any substance eaten or drunk by a pregnant woman will end up in her baby's bloodstream. (ii) At what stages during a baby's development would high levels of alcohol in the mother's blood be dangerous? (Level 7)

Binge drinking

Scientists have recently discovered more about the problems of **binge drinking**, especially for young people. They have estimated that binge drinking costs the NHS £1.7 billion a year. Public advertisements are targeted at young people, showing them the dangers that they face when they drink too much alcohol.

E   Some scientists have stated that if alcohol was discovered now it would be classified as a harmful and illegal substance. With reference to the health and social effects of drinking, explain why this might be the case. (Level 8)

Newsflash

The number of people becoming addicted to medical drugs which they can buy over the Internet, such as anti-depressants and painkillers, is increasing. Deaths from the misuse of these drugs have doubled in the last ten years.

causes liver damage
—
loss of balance
—
makes you sleepy
—
slows your reactions
—
affects your judgement
—
loss of inhibitions
—
blurred vision

▲ How does alcohol affect the body?

▲ Know your limits

Keywords
binge drinking, drug, illegal drug, medical drug, legal drug, withdrawal symptom

It's a matter of class

Learn about:

- how and why drugs are classified
- the social effects of the drugs trade
- how science helps people make informed decisions

▲ About 90% of the heroin on British streets is produced in Afghanistan

In 1961 illegal drugs were classified by the government, based on how dangerous scientists thought they were. Class A drugs were the most dangerous, followed by Class B, with Class C being the least. Possession of these illegal drugs carries a prison sentence.

The maximum prison sentences for drug possession	Class A	Class B	Class C
possession	7 years	5 years	2 years
supplying	life	14 years	5 years

Drug	Effects	Side effects	Class	Top 20 ranking of the most harmful
heroin	euphoria (a feeling of well being and happiness)	very addictive easy to overdose	A	1
cocaine	alert, confident stimulant	very addictive	A	2
alcohol	relaxed euphoria	depression sedative heart and liver damage	U*	5
speed (amphetamines)	increased energy	paranoia depression	B	8
nicotine	relaxed	very addictive cancer	U*	9
cannabis	euphoria relaxed pain relief	paranoia memory loss lung cancer	C	11
LSD	euphoria hallucinations	bad 'trips'	A	14
ecstasy	increased energy hallucinations	dehydration loss of memory	A	18

* U = unclassified – it is legal to be in possession of and buy these drugs, providing you are over the age limit

Until recently, the government's **drug classifications** remained the same. In 2004 cannabis was reclassified from a Class B to a Class C drug. This was due to new scientific evidence on its effects. The research supported the original theory that cannabis was harmful, but found it was not as harmful as some other Class B drugs.

A If you are found in possession of a small amount of cannabis, what is the maximum prison sentence you can expect? (Level 4)

New research

Recent scientific research has produced a new list of the top 20 most harmful drugs: 1 being most harmful and 20 being least harmful. The order is based on scientific evidence of the effects of the drug, how addictive it is and the consequences of using this drug on society. The study shows some surprising results.

B Alcohol, an unclassified drug, has been classed as the fifth most harmful drug. Suggest why. (Level 5)

C There is a wide difference in the classification of some drugs compared to what scientists think their potential harm is. Make a list of those with the largest difference and explain why this is the case. (Level 6)

Drugs and society

The drug trade has a huge impact worldwide. It is linked to crime, poverty and abuse of human rights.

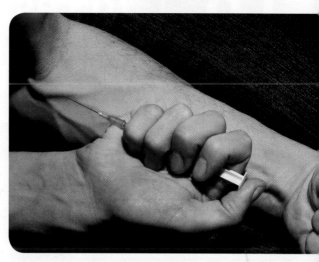

▲ Addicts often become involved in crime to pay for drugs

Police Statement

On 22 May, John Smith was caught breaking and entering a house. On arrest he appeared pale, agitated and covered in sweat. When questioned about why he had committed the crime he replied: 'I need money for heroin, I'm desperate.' John had been addicted to heroin for 18 months. He was unemployed, had sold all of his belongings and lived in a squat.

A South American woman was rushed to hospital yesterday and is fighting for her life after collapsing at Gatwick airport. Ten packages of cocaine were found in her stomach, one of which had burst. It is thought she was paid to smuggle drugs for a major drug supplier in Columbia.

D Think about the two examples of the social impact of drugs described above. What others can you think of? (Level 7)

Science at work

Forensic scientists are often involved in bringing drug dealers and traffickers to justice. They analyse drugs found at crime scenes to find out what they are.

E Governments spend millions on advertisements and campaigns to make people more drug aware. What role does science play in this? (Level 8)

0800 77 66 00   talktofrank.com

◀ New initiatives, like the Frank helpline are introduced to make young people aware of the harm drugs cause

Keywords
drug classification

11

1.6 To test or not to test?

Learn about:
- the stages involved in the testing of a new drug
- why scientists test medical drugs on animals
- what can happen when testing goes wrong

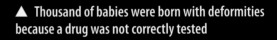

Stage 1
Drugs are tested on tissue cultures. Tissue cultures are small groups of animal or human cells grown in the laboratory.

Stage 2
Animal testing is carried out using rats, mice, dogs and monkeys. Scientists will see if the drug actually works and if there are any **side effects**. They test animals at different stages of their life cycles to see if there is any difference in response. Scientists have to be aware that animals may not respond to the drugs in the same way as humans.

Stage 3
Clinical trials are carried out. A small group of healthy human volunteers is given the drug and observed to see if any side effects occur. If this is successful then the drug will be given to larger groups and to volunteers suffering from the illness. Scientists will compare how effective the drug is compared to existing treatments. Scientists also work out the dose that needs to be given for the drug to work. Not all volunteers are given the drug. Some are given dummy drugs called **placebos**. This is to ensure that any effects seen are due to the drug and not some other factor.

▲ Thousand of babies were born with deformities because a drug was not correctly tested

Thalidomide was given to pregnant women in the 1950s as a drug to treat morning sickness. As a direct result, 10,000 babies were born with severely deformed limbs. Thalidomide had not been tested on pregnant animals so scientists didn't know what harm it would cause to unborn offspring.

From laboratory to pharmacy
Drugs have to be extensively tested before they are licensed to go on sale to make sure they work and are safe. There are three main stages in licensing a drug.

▲ Asthma inhalers were developed using animal testing

> I don't agree with animal testing, it's cruel.

> But without it thousands of people would suffer.

Interesting fact

Drug testing is a lengthy and expensive process. Only one in every 10 000 medical drugs developed will make it on to the market and it can cost up to £400 million to get it to market.

A Why is it important to carry out testing on drugs before releasing them onto the market? (Level 4)

B Why is it important to test drugs on animals at different stages in their life cycle? (Level 5)

When things go wrong

Making sure that a drug is safe for use is a complicated process involving several stages. As you have already seen, this process can go wrong.

Drug trial goes wrong

In 2006, clinical trials on an anti-inflammatory drug went wrong. Six volunteers suffered a severe reaction to it. Their **immune systems** started attacking their internal organs and their bodies swelled up. The drug had been tested on animals with no major side effects, but it had a terrible effect on the human body.

C If animal testing was banned (i) what might happen to volunteers in clinical trials? (ii) what might happen to the number of people willing to undergo clinical trials and why? (Level 6)

D (i) Why is it necessary to carry out clinical trials on humans? (ii) What could the scientists have done to minimise the risks in the clinical trial that went wrong? (Level 7)

Should drugs be tested on animals?

Many people feel that we should not abuse the rights of animals and that all animal testing should be banned. Others feel that it is essential to find cures for the many diseases from which humans suffer. Some diseases still have no cure and many scientists think that animal testing is essential.

Where possible, scientists use cells grown in laboratories instead of animals. However, it is British law that any new drug intended for use as a medicine must be tested on two different species of mammal.

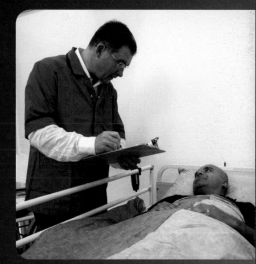

▲ People are paid to be human 'guinea pigs'

E Produce a table listing the arguments for and against animal testing. (Level 8)

Keywords
animal testing, clinical trial, immune system, placebo, side effect, thalidomide

Moving and grooving

Learn about:

- why you have a skeleton and how you move it
- how exercise affects movement
- how science can help to keep you mobile

▶ Arthritis is a common illness in elderly people, but can be helped with replacement joints

Connie has developed **arthritis** in her hip joint. Cartilage between the joint in her hip has worn away and without this cushion her bones rub together causing pain and affecting her ability to walk. Her doctor has offered her a replacement hip joint.

A What two bones will Connie have a replacement joint between? (Level 4)

Structurally sound

Without **bones** you would have no structure to your body. You would have nothing to protect your internal organs and you wouldn't be able to move. The **skeleton** in the human body is made up of about 206 bones. Bones are strong and are living tissue, so they have a good blood supply. This is why they can heal if you break one.

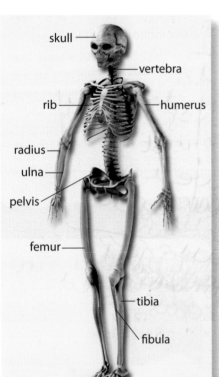

◀ The human skeleton

skull
vertebra
rib
humerus
radius
ulna
pelvis
femur
tibia
fibula

B Which bones protect your lungs and heart? (Level 5)

Socket to 'em

There are several types of joints between the bones. The joints allow bones to move freely against each other.

Your elbow is a **hinge joint**. It is called a hinge joint because it works a bit like a door hinge. Hinge joints allow bones to move backwards and forwards, a bit like opening and closing a door.

Your shoulder is a **ball and socket joint**. These are the most mobile type of joint in the human body and allow you to swing your arms and legs in many different directions.

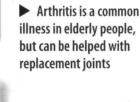

cartilage
femur
synovial fluid
tibia

▲ A hinge joint

▼ A ball and socket joint

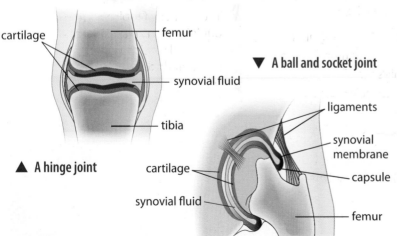

ligaments
synovial membrane
capsule
cartilage
synovial fluid
femur

C Where else in the body would you find a hinge joint and a ball and socket joint? (Level 6)

▶ The socket is attached to the hip and the ball is attached to the femur

Artificial joints

Doctors will remove Connie's worn out hip joint and replace it with an artificial one made of metal and plastic. The joint is cemented and screwed onto Connie's bones and can last for up to 20 years. Artificial joints can have the same mobility and strength as an original joint.

On the move

You wouldn't be able to move your joints without your muscles. It is the contraction and relaxation of muscles that help you bend and move your joints.

The muscles in your arms are called an **antagonistic pair**. This is because they work together but pull in opposite directions. Muscles can only pull, they cannot push. When your **biceps** contracts, your **triceps** relaxes, and when your triceps contracts, your biceps relaxes.

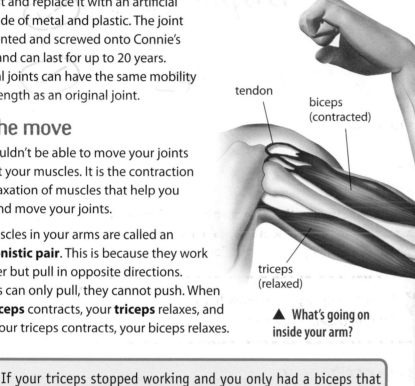

tendon

biceps (contracted)

tendon

triceps (relaxed)

▲ What's going on inside your arm?

D If your triceps stopped working and you only had a biceps that pulled, describe the range of movement your arm would have and why it would move like this. (Level 7)

Keeping supple

Once Connie has had her operation she will need some **physiotherapy** to help her muscles and joint to work properly again. Physiotherapists treat patients with a range of problems resulting from illness or injury. They help to restore muscles and joints back to full fitness through therapy and exercise.

Exercise keeps muscles toned and increases their strength. It keeps the joints working smoothly and helps maintain an efficient blood supply to muscles and bones. An exercise programme will play a key part in Connie's recovery as it will help heal and strengthen the new joint. She will also need to make sure she takes in plenty of calcium to keep her bones strong.

E Being overweight can lead to osteoarthritis. Osteoarthritis is a condition in which cartilage is worn away. (i) Why may this eventually lead to a sufferer needing an artificial joint? (ii) Which types of joints will this condition be more common in? (Level 8)

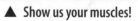
▲ Show us your muscles!

Science at work

The science of replacing a worn out joint with an artificial one is continually being developed. At the moment doctors can replace the shoulder, elbow, hip, knee, ankle, and certain joints in the hand.

Keywords

antagonistic pair, arthritis, ball and socket joint, biceps, bone, hinge joint, physiotherapy, skeleton, triceps

1.8 Finger gym

Best Science Lesson Ever

Learn about:

- how rest is an important part of exercise
- the most effective way for athletes to train

▲ Top athletes need to be physically 'fit' and have lots of energy

Top athletes can build up their stamina and strength with regular exercise. The more an Olympic athlete trains, the shorter their recovery time and the less fatigued they feel. But it is important for them to train in the right way.

You have already seen in *Go Science! 2* that **aerobic respiration** is the process by which oxygen and glucose are used to produce energy. At finger gym, you will be seeing if your energy levels are higher if you have regular periods of rest between finger weightlifting.

Before you start

Like all athletes, you will need a personal coach to help you during your workout. One person will be the weightlifter and the other will be the coach. The coach's job is to encourage the person training, keep time and record the results.

The weightlifter is going to be doing five sets of weightlifting for three minutes with five minute breaks in between each set. For each set of exercise, the amount of rest during the three minutes of exercise will increase. You are testing if resting between exercise helps you increase the number of finger weightlifts you can do.

A How do oxygen and glucose get into your body? (Level 4)

What you will need

You will need for each pair:

- stop watch
- 100 g weights
- sticky tape.

What to do – weight lifter

①

Attach a 100 g weight to the right index finger (the top third of the finger) securely with sticky tape.

②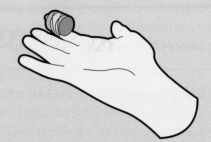

Place your hand flat on the desk, palm upwards.

3

Lift the weight as often as possible for three minutes. Your coach will record the number of lifts you do per minute for three minutes. Rest your finger for five minutes.

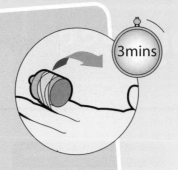

4

Lift the weight as often as possible for three minutes, but this time your coach will give you 30 seconds rest between each minute of exercise. Rest your finger for five minutes.

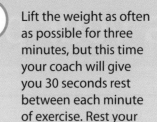

Repeat with 60, 90 and 120 seconds rest between each minute of exercise in each three minute set.

B What must you keep the same in this experiment to make it a fair test? (Level 5)

C How could you make this experiment reliable? (Level 6)

What to do – coach

1 Check the weightlifter carries out the exercise correctly.

2 Measure the time intervals for the weightlifter.

3 Your teacher will give you a copy of a results table. Record the data in a copy of the table.

Interesting fact

An athlete's diet is very important. Athletes achieve peak performance by eating a variety of food, but they get the most energy from carbohydrates such as pasta, potatoes and cereals.

Is rest best?

When you exercise you need more energy, so you respire at a faster rate. Sometimes your body cannot take in enough oxygen for the energy demand and your cells respire without oxygen – **anaerobic respiration**. When this happens you produce lactic acid in your body.

If you exercise your muscles for too long without rest you get tired. Muscle 'burn' is caused by a build up of lactic acid. This is called **muscle fatigue**.

Following periods of rest, the muscles in your finger recover from fatigue. The longer the rest the better the recovery and the higher the number of finger weight lifts.

D When you are pumping iron at finger gym, why might you start to respire without oxygen? (Level 7)

E If you were competing at finger weightlifting against a world class athlete, how would you expect your performance to differ and how can you explain these differences? (Level 8)

Keywords
aerobic respiration, anaerobic respiration, muscle fatigue

Voted a Best Lesson at St. Teilo's Church-in-Wales High School

Assess your progress

1.2

1. What is fitness a measure of? (Level 4)
2. Apart from taking regular exercise, what else must you do to ensure a healthy lifestyle? (Level 5)
3. Oxygen is needed for respiration in active cells. Write down the word equation for respiration. (Level 6)
4. Think about your lifestyle. What three changes could you make to make yourself fitter? (Level 7)
5.

fruit and vegetables

bread, rice, potatoes, cereals and pasta

FLAKES

milk and dairy foods

foods and drinks high in fats and/or sugar

meat, fish, eggs and beans

Comparison of fitness training

Fitness type	Calories per day	Major food group	Daily exercise
	3800	protein	weight training 3 hours a day 6 days a week
	2900	protein	running and gym 5 hours a day 6 days a week
	2500	carbohydrate balanced diet	30 minutes moderate exercise 5 days a week

The diagram shows the nutrients in a balanced diet. Bodybuilders often take a diet supplement in the form of a drink or tablet.
a Which nutrient would this contain an excess of?
b Why do they do this?
c What foods could they eat instead of this? (Level 8)

1.3

1. What is in a cigarette that damages the lining of the trachea? (Level 4)
2. Give three medical reasons why you shouldn't smoke. (Level 5)
3.

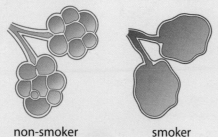

non-smoker   smoker

a Look at the diagram comparing the alveoli of a smoker and non-smoker. What does smoking do to the surface area of the lungs available for gas exchange?
b What would be the effects of this in terms of:
(i) oxygen levels in blood;
(ii) carbon dioxide levels in blood? (Level 6)

4. How have advances in science helped reduce the number of people who die from smoking? (Level 7)
5. Nicotine patches contain a small amount of nicotine and help people give up smoking. a
a Why is wearing a nicotine patch less harmful than smoking?
b Nicotine is an addictive substance. What does this mean?
c What should people do to make sure they do not become addicted to the nicotine patches? (Level 8)

1.4

1. List the three groups of drugs and give one example of each. (Level 4)
2. Why has the government classified some drugs as illegal? (Level 5)
3. Drug use has been taking place for thousands of years but has only been made illegal in the last century or so – why do you think this is? (Level 6)
4. What drugs should a woman avoid if she is trying to become pregnant? (Level 7)
5. Coffee contains the drug caffeine.
   a Why do some people feel they cannot start the day without a cup of coffee?
   b Caffeine makes you need to pass urine more frequently. What effect would this have on your body and how would this affect your caffeine intake? (Level 8)

1.5

1. Cannabis has been reclassified from B to C. Does this make it legal? (Level 4)
2. Taking ecstasy gives you lots of energy. Why may this lead to dehydration? (Level 5)
3. Look at the table of drugs. Given the ranking of drugs by scientists, how would you re-classify drugs? Produce a table showing your classification. (Level 6)
4. Cannabis is often used for pain relief. Do you think cannabis should be declassified/made legal? Give reasons for your answer. (Level 7)
5. The illegal drugs industry involves law breaking on many levels.
   a From the source to the street, list as many illegal acts that take place as you can.
   b What drives the people involved to take such a risk? (Level 8)

Drug	Effects	Side effects	Class	Top 20 ranking of the most harmful
heroin	euphoria (a feeling of well being and happiness)	very addictive easy to overdose	A	1
cocaine	alert, confident stimulant	very addictive	A	2
alcohol	relaxed euphoria	depression sedative heart and liver damage	U*	5
speed (amphetamines)	increased energy	paranoia depression	B	8
nicotine	relaxed	very addictive cancer	U*	9
cannabis	euphoria relaxed pain relief	paranoia memory loss lung cancer	C	11
LSD	euphoria hallucinations	bad 'trips'	A	14
ecstasy	increased energy hallucinations	dehydration loss of memory	A	18

* U = unclassified – it is legal to be in possession of and buy these drugs, providing you are over the age limit

Assess your progress

1.6

1 What are the three stages of a drugs trial? (Level 4)

2 Why do you think so few drugs that are developed gain a licence to be sold? (Level 5)

3 According to British law, drugs must be tested on two species of animal, one of which is a non-rodent. Suggest why this is. (Level 6)

4 Suggest why animal testing is a subject that provokes such strong feelings in people. (Level 7)

5 In clinical trials, some people are given a placebo.
   a Why is this done?
   b Look at the graph of results of a clinical trial.

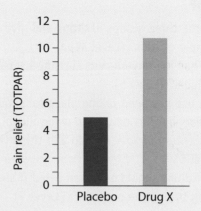

   What happened to those that took the placebo?
   c This is called the placebo effect. Suggest why this occasionally happens. (Level 8)

1.7

1 What disease can make joints very painful and affect movement. (Level 4)

2 Why do we need a skeleton? (Level 5)

3 Look at the diagram of the arm and describe the movement of your triceps and biceps when lifting an object and then putting it down again. (Level 6)

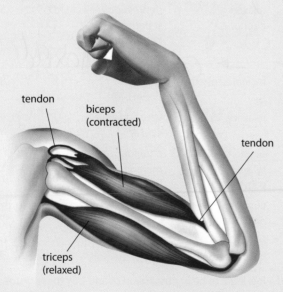

tendon

biceps (contracted)

tendon

triceps (relaxed)

4 What type of joint do you have in your elbow? Describe the range of movement you would have in your arm if you had a ball and socket joint instead. (Level 7)

5 Scientists are currently spending a lot of time and money developing joint replacement treatments. Why are they doing this? (Level 8)

1.8

1 Your gym coach is eager for you to do more training. If you were to repeat the finger gym experiment, how would you improve it? (Level 4)

2 At finger gym, your pulse can race. Why does your heart rate increase during exercise?

(Level 5)

3 The coaches notice that some finger weight lifters do more lifts per minute than others. Why might this be the case? (Level 6)

4 Why do top athletes have lower pulse and breathing rates? (Level 7)

5 Were there any anomalies in your results? How can you explain them? (Level 8)

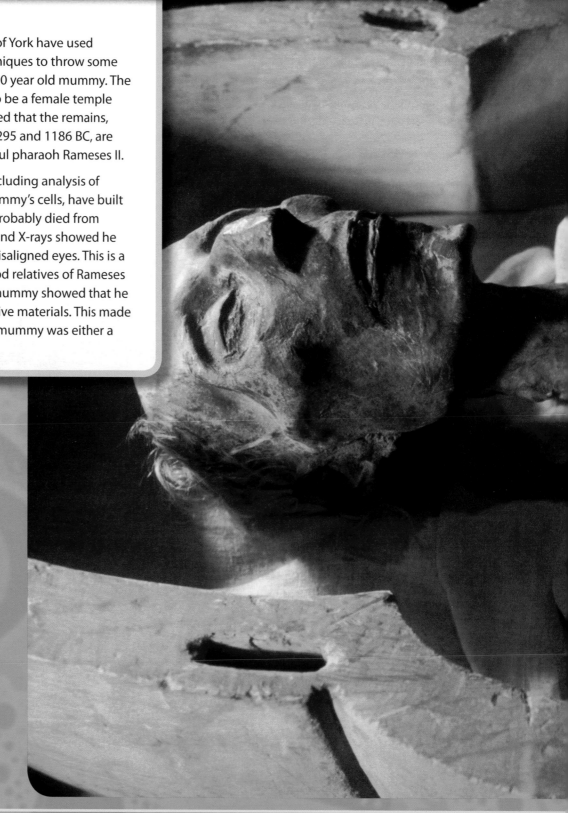

2.1 Scientific evidence

A team from the University of York have used cutting-edge scientific techniques to throw some light on the identity of a 3000 year old mummy. The mummy was first thought to be a female temple dancer. Scientists have proved that the remains, which date from between 1295 and 1186 BC, are those of a son of the powerful pharaoh Rameses II.

The scientific techniques, including analysis of inherited material in the mummy's cells, have built up a picture of a man who probably died from cancer in his thirties. Scans and X-rays showed he had a misaligned jaw and misaligned eyes. This is a feature shared by many blood relatives of Rameses II. Chemical analysis of the mummy showed that he was embalmed with expensive materials. This made the scientists think that the mummy was either a priest or from a royal family.

Now try these

- Write a short paragraph explaining what you know about inherited features.

- Biologists and chemists work in different areas of science but they worked together to solve the mystery of the mummy. Explain the part that each played in the investigation.

- Choose a family. Draw a family tree to show some members of the family. Add some information about each of the people you have included.

Coming up in this Chapter ...

Members of the same family have features in common because they share many of the same genes

Dog breeders choose dogs with particular features and breed them together

Sportspeople have natural ability but they still have to practise

Crops with special features could help to feed the world

Learn about:

- the differences between sexual and asexual reproduction
- why variation in a species is useful
- how you can use models to help you understand variation

▶ Bacteria reproduce very rapidly

A **bacteriologist** studies microbes. Single-celled organisms such as bacteria reproduce by splitting in half. This type of reproduction is called **asexual reproduction**. One bacterium can produce millions of offspring in a very short time in warm, moist conditions with food available.

No matter how many offspring are produced they will all be identical to the parent bacterium. This is because the new bacteria have the same **genetic material** as their parent. Asexual reproduction happens in more complicated animals and plants as well, such as strawberry plants and some worms. The offspring are always identical to the parent.

A A bacteriologist studies a new type of bacterium under the microscope. Their conditions are warm and moist and they have a food source. Suggest what he might notice about the offspring of the bacteria he is studying. (Level 4)

▲ A litter of kittens may have different coloured coats and different eye colours

The same but different

Many living things have offspring which are not identical to their parents. The parents and offspring have some similarities and some differences. Scientists call these differences **variation**.

Variation may help a species to survive. Some individuals may inherit features from their parents which help them to survive when conditions get difficult and others die.

B Why is it an advantage for individuals of the same species to have some differences? (Level 5)

Sperm and eggs

Sexual reproduction involves combining genetic material from two parents. This happens when the nuclei of a sperm and an egg join together. Sperm and eggs are specialised sex cells and contain half the number of genes that are found in your other cells. Every sperm and every egg contains a different set of genes.

The nucleus of every cell in your body contains genetic information in the **genes** and your genes give you your features.

stigma – where pollen grains land

style – holds up the stigma

anther – part of the stamen that makes pollen grains

carpel – female organ

stamen – male organ

ovary – makes egg cells

petal – attracts bees

Every individual inherits a different combination of genes from their parents, and as a result every individual is different. Many animals reproduce sexually – genes from the parents are mixed and the offspring show variation.

C Explain why sperm and eggs contain only half the amount of genetic material that is found in the other cells of an organism? (Level 6)

Plant reproduction

Like animals, when plants reproduce sexually the offspring show variation. This is because genetic material from two nuclei is combined. The male sex cell (**pollen grain**) is carried to the stigma by wind or insects. It develops a **pollen tube** which grows down the style and into the ovule. The nucleus from the grain then travels down the tube to fuse with the nucleus of the female cell (**ovum**) present in the ovule. This process is called **pollination** and seeds are produced which may, one day, become new plants.

Variation model

The prize in the school raffle is a television and Tom wants to win it. 'You can buy one ticket for £1 or a book of six tickets for £5,' he says. 'I need to buy a book of tickets. With six tickets I have more chance of having the winning ticket.'

Mr Philips tells his pupils, 'Variation between members of the same species is rather like buying ten different lottery tickets each week in an attempt to win the lottery, compared with buying just one'.

D Explain how Tom's statement about buying raffle tickets might be used as a model of variation. (Level 7)

E Mr Philips goes on to tell his pupils he has noticed that when the weather has been poor, the plants in his garden produce lots of flowers which produce lots of seeds. Use the lottery model to explain his observation. (Level 8)

Interesting fact

Scientists estimate that as much as one third of the human diet comes from plants which are pollinated by insects. Eighty percent of this pollination is carried out by honey bees but these bees are experiencing a worrying drop in their numbers. It is vital that scientists discover the reasons for this so that they can do something to stop the decline.

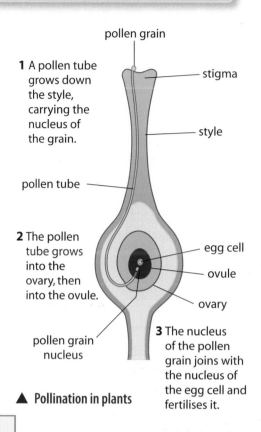

pollen grain

1 A pollen tube grows down the style, carrying the nucleus of the grain.

stigma

style

pollen tube

2 The pollen tube grows into the ovary, then into the ovule.

egg cell

ovule

ovary

pollen grain nucleus

3 The nucleus of the pollen grain joins with the nucleus of the egg cell and fertilises it.

▲ **Pollination in plants**

▲ **A hawk which inherits sharp claws and good eyesight from its parents will be a successful hunter. If these features are particularly good, it may be able to catch prey that other hawks can't**

Keywords
asexual reproduction, bacteriologist, gene, genetic material, ovum, pollen grain, pollen tube, pollination, sexual reproduction, variation

2.3 Investigating features

Learn about:

- how the environment influences features
- why scientists study twins
- what affects plant features

▶ **Chang and Eng were the original Siamese twins and were born in Siam in 1811**

A Explain why identical twins have the same genes. (Level 4)

Interesting fact

Conjoined twins have differences even though they are identical and share the same environment. Chang was an alcoholic while Eng was a good poker player. They often fell out with each other and had big arguments!

Identical twins are formed when a fertilised egg splits in two and the two parts go on to become two individuals. In **conjoined twins**, such as Chang and Eng, the split is not complete and the two individuals are joined. Because they come from the same egg and sperm each pair of conjoined twins and identical twins has the same genes.

What affects your features?

You have already seen that you inherit genes from both your parents and that these genes control your features. They control whether you have:

- a big nose or a small nose
- straight hair or curly hair
- green eyes or brown eyes
- and many other things too!

Most scientists think that inheritance and environment act together to produce some of a person's features. But scientists often disagree about how important each influence is in producing a feature. The table shows some features.

Genes, environment or both?

Influenced by environment	Influenced by genes and environment	Influenced by genes
language	skin colour	eye colour
religion	height	blood type
	weight	

Obesity is a growing health problem in the UK. Most scientists think that diet and exercise are important factors but they are also interested in the part played by genes.

Some scientists now believe that they have discovered two 'fat' genes that influence a person's weight. They think that people who inherit these genes tend to have more body fat and put on weight more easily than people who do not carry the genes but have a similar lifestyle. Science is exploring how genes and body weight are linked but there are no definite answers yet.

B (i) Identify the two factors/influences that affect an individual's features. (ii) Outline the different opinions that scientists have about how these two factors affect features. (Level 5)

Studying twins

Scientists have studied identical twins who have been separated as children and brought up in different families. They share the same genes although their environments are different. Studying these identical twins can give scientists information about how features are influenced by the environment.

I have sisters who are non-identical twins and girl cousins who are identical twins. My cousins are much more alike than my sisters are. I don't understand it – they are both twins!

▲ Identical twins may both inherit the genes for tallness

▲ One twin has a poorer diet than the other

▲ The twin with the healthier diet may grow taller

C (i) Explain to Sam why his cousins are more alike than his sisters. (ii) His teacher tells him that identical twins are always the same sex. Explain this as well. (Level 6)

D Explain how a scientist might use twins to look at how genes and the environment influence heart disease. (Level 7)

Plant features

Plants also carry genes which give them their features. Their structure, leaf shape and flower colour are some of the features determined by their genes, but their environment is also important. Plants need light, carbon dioxide and water to **photosynthesise**. They also need **nutrients** from the soil to grow. If these are lacking in the environment the plant will not grow well and may have pale or poorly developed leaves, flowers and stems.

E Sophie takes cuttings from a plant and grows them all in the same type of soil. The cuttings are all the same size and have the same number of leaves. (i) Describe an experiment that Sophie can do to investigate the effect that different levels of light in the environment will have on her plants. (ii) Explain how using cuttings grown and selected in this way will enable her to obtain a reliable result in her investigation. (Level 8)

▲ A healthy grapevine and (below) one lacking magnesium

Keywords
conjoined twins, identical twins, nutrients, photosynthesise

27

Investigating behaviour

Learn about:

- how psychologists disagree about how behaviour develops
- why social behaviours are useful
- why it is difficult to study human behaviour

▲ Learning about learning

Interesting fact

Although they have identical genes, identical twins may not have the same fingerprints. This is because there is an environmental influence on how fingertips develop and the environment in the womb is not exactly the same for each twin as they develop.

Psychologists are scientists who are interested in how humans behave. They have different opinions about what influences the ways that humans think, learn and behave. They do not always agree exactly on the part played by genes and the part played by environment.

> **A** Why might psychologists be interested in the way that young children learn? (Level 4)

Twins again

Pairs of identical twins have been studied by scientists interested in how personality develops. Comparing these twins with randomly selected pairs of individuals with different genes, they found that identical twins have personalities which are much more similar. These similarities are due to their identical genes.

Identical twins have the same genes but if they are brought up apart their environment will have been different. Non-identical twins, brought up together, have different genes but their environment is likely to have been much more similar. Looking at pairs of twins like these and comparing them may help scientists to decide which features are inherited and which are due to the environment.

> **B** Suggest what the scientists concluded from the investigation into twins' personalities. (Level 5)

▲ Seeing double

Studying twins has helped scientists at Kings College London university find out about the genes involved in baldness in men. They studied identical twins and other unrelated men to see which men lost their hair at a young age and now think that hair loss is controlled by more than one gene. This may help them to eventually prevent this hair loss.

▲ Humans learn by being with other humans

C Identical twins are the same genetically, having developed from one sperm and one egg. They may share the same placenta in the uterus. Scientists know that sometimes one twin is better positioned in the uterus than the other and receives better nutrition. (i) What effect might this have on the development of the twins and their weight and body length at birth? (ii) How might a low birth weight affect the way that the twin develops after birth? (Level 6)

Learning how to behave

Humans live in groups and need to know how to behave correctly in different social situations so that they fit in. They learn from other members of the group by observing and by being taught what to do.

Humans start to learn the rules of behaviour at a young age and take a long time to grow up compared to other animals. Psychologists believe that this is because humans have such a lot to learn, including language.

D Explain why a human's ability to use language is so important in their development. (Level 7)

Designing behaviour experiments

In the early 1960s in the USA, Stanley Milgram investigated how obedient humans are. He set up a fake experiment in which he asked volunteers to give electric shocks to 'subjects' who were learning word pairs. When the 'subjects' got these wrong, they were given a shock by the volunteers.

The 'subjects' were actors and were not actually receiving an electric shock, just pretending that they were. The volunteers believed that they were hurting the 'subjects', yet 65% of them gave the 'subjects' the maximum, but fake, shock.

Milgram showed that volunteers are often keen to do what scientists ask, even something they would normally think was wrong. He also showed that it is necessary to design investigations so that the people taking part do not know what the scientists are investigating as they may change their behaviour because of this.

▲ Rorschach inkblots tests were once used by some psychologists to test personality. These unclear images were created in 1921 and it was thought that a subject's responses to the images could help the psychologists assess what type of personality a person has

E Explain why Milgram's experiment was so influential in the study of human behaviour and suggest why other scientists were so surprised by the results. (Level 8)

Keywords
nature, nurture, personality, psychologist

Learn about:

- why animal breeders and farmers use selective breeding
- how selective breeding is carried out
- the ethical issues associated with selective breeding

▲ Fast-growing food

Forty years ago, it took nearly three months for a chicken to be fully grown and ready for the oven. Less than 8 billion chickens were eaten worldwide then, compared with 49 billion today.

Nowadays, chickens grow to eating size in record time. Farmers breed fast-growing chickens with other fast-growing chickens to produce the meat much more quickly. This process, in which animals with **desirable features** are bred with each other over generations, is called **selective breeding**.

A   What do scientists mean by the term selective breeding? (Level 4)

▲ Belgian Blues are the muscled giants of the cow world

Food for thought

Scientists have selectively bred lots of different farm animals, including chickens that produce more eggs and cows that produce more milk and meat.

Belgian Blues are enormous cattle kept for meat. The original Belgian Blues were bred with Shorthorn beef cattle. A change happened to the genes of some of their offspring which produced extra muscle in the cattle. By breeding these 'double muscled' animals together, generation after generation, farmers produced giant meat producers. Unfortunately, the extra muscle of Belgian blues makes it difficult for them to give birth.

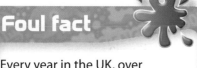

Foul fact

Every year in the UK, over 30 million day-old male chicks are killed. The males are no use as egg layers and because these chickens have been bred to produce eggs, the chicks do not grow up fast enough or meaty enough to produce meat.

B   Modern chickens are descended from jungle fowls. Suggest how selective breeding has changed the original jungle fowl into a modern meat or egg-producing chicken. (Level 5)

C For each of the following, give a feature that has been bred into the animal through selective breeding: (i) dairy cow (ii) beef cow (iii) meat-producing chicken (iv) egg-producing chicken. (Level 6)

Ethical issues

Some people think that selective breeding is a good idea because increased food production is good for the human population. Other people think it is a bad idea because in some cases selective breeding creates problems for the animals.

Belgian Blue cattle produce such large calves that they have to be born by caesarean. Meat-producing chickens put on weight so quickly that their hearts and their bones are put under strain and it is likely that they suffer pain as a result. Some may die from heart failure. Strangely it may be possible to put many of these problems right using more selective breeding.

▲ Compassion in World Farming (CIWF) encourages people to think about the welfare issues associated with keeping and breeding animals. Veterinary surgeons visit farms to check on the health of the animals

D Suggest advantages and ethical issues of selectively breeding: (i) people who are good at science (ii) apples resistant to pests and disease (iii) pigs that have large litters of piglets (iv) hairless cats. (Level 7)

E Male calves born to cows that have been selectively bred as dairy cows are no use for milk production. (i) Explain why this is the case. (ii) Some of the calves are kept to produce veal. In your opinion does this solve the animal welfare issues associated with selective breeding? (Level 8)

▲ Belted Galloway cattle are a rare breed which are now making a comeback

Selective breeding and the environment

Scientists agree that it is important to have a wide variety of animals and plants in the environment. They call this **biodiversity**. Plants and animals rely on each other in many different ways and if the number and variety of organisms decreases these relationships are disrupted.

Selective breeding can reduce biodiversity. It can lead to organisms becoming rare or extinct because they have features which are not as desirable as selectively bred organisms. Other animals which rely on these organisms will be affected too.

Keywords
biodiversity, desirable feature, selective breeding

Learn about:

- how the features of an organism can be changed by changing its genes
- why genetic engineering is useful
- potential problems with GM

▲ Is this Frankenstein science?

This mouse has been given a gene from a jellyfish which makes the mouse emit a green glow. The mouse has been **genetically modified (GM)**. Scientists knew that the experiment had worked when they saw that the mouse glowed under ultraviolet light.

Genetic engineering

Scientists can take a gene from one species and put into another. They are now able to select the piece of genetic material that is responsible for a particular feature, cut it out and transfer it to the cells of another organism. They do this to give an organism desirable features. The process is called **genetic engineering** and it is complex and expensive to carry out. Scientists call organisms which have been given genes from another living thing **transgenic**.

Interesting fact

A transgenic animal has some genes which have come from another species and is sometimes called a chimera. This name comes from a monster in Greek mythology that had a lion's head, a goat's body and a serpent's tail.

Some media articles sensationalise genetic engineering. They pick unusual experiments to write about and do not always allow scientists to explain all of the science behind them.

Scientists create a sheep that is 15% human!

A
(i) What does the term transgenic mean?
(ii) What does GM stand for? (Level 4)

Plants for food

Plants can also be genetically modified. Scientists can transfer disease-resistant genes or pest-resistant genes from one plant to create disease-resistant or pest-resistant crops. Gene transfer has also been used to make some crops resistant to weedkiller. The farmer can then spray the crops with weedkiller and only the weeds will die.

Vitamin A is lacking in the diets of people in some countries and they go blind as a result. Genetic engineering can be used to produce a type of rice which contains vitamin A and can prevent this problem. It is called 'golden rice'.

B (i) Why is golden rice useful? (ii) What has been done to the genes of ordinary rice to produce golden rice? (Level 5)

GM humans

Scientists may be able to use genetic engineering to cure diseases by cutting out damaged genes and replacing them with healthy genes. Scientists may also be able to grow human organs for transplant using transgenic donor animals.

▲ Golden rice contains vitamin A

Could GM athletes be bred to run faster marathons?

Sports scientists believe that no more new records will be set after 2060 because by then athletes will have reached the end of human capability. Only genetic changes to their organs will allow them to go faster.

Some scientists believe that genetic engineering may be able to produce super athletes in the future with the ability to complete the 26.2 mile marathon course in 90 minutes.

C Do you think that creating super athletes is a worthwhile use of genetic engineering? Explain your answer. (Level 6)

Pros and cons

Genetic engineering does not always work but when it does, it produces change quickly. It can produce fast-growing salmon much more quickly than selective breeding can. Scientists need to think carefully about what might go wrong before any experiments are carried out.

- Transgenic animals might escape and breed with animals in the wild. This could be a problem because the new species might compete with natural organisms for resources and threaten their survival. The introduced gene might make the new species impossible to control if it becomes a threat.
- Transgenic pollen might be blown in the wind and pollinate wild plants. It might be impossible to kill weeds with weedkiller if they pick up a weedkiller-resistant gene from a nearby GM crop.

▲ Paula Radcliffe's marathon record was 2 hours 15 minutes 25 seconds

D Explain why scientists put genetically modified crops in fields with a large 'buffer zone' of uncultivated land around the field. (Level 7)

E Scientists often tell the public that their GM organisms are sterile and unable to breed with unmodified organisms. (i) Explain why this is an important safety precaution. (ii) Who do you think should control what the scientists are allowed to do in their GM experiments? (Level 8)

Keywords
genetic engineering, genetically modified (GM), transgenic

2.7 Creating a copy

Learn about:
- what a clone is
- why scientists have produced clones and how they do it
- the moral and ethical issues with cloning humans

▲ So good they made it twice!

The cat in the photo, Copy Cat, was born on 22 December 2001 in Texas in the USA. She was special because she was the first pet animal to be cloned.

What is a clone?

A **clone** is an exact genetic copy of an animal or plant. Nature often makes clones when it produces identical twins and when plants and animals reproduce asexually.

Over a number of years, scientists developed a procedure that enabled them to clone animals. Dolly the sheep, born in 1997 after 276 attempts, was the first large mammal to be cloned. Since then several species of animals have been cloned including horses, pigs and goats.

A Explain what is meant by the scientific term 'clone'. (Level 4)

Gardeners have been cloning their favourite plants for years by taking stem cuttings and planting them. A new African violet plant will grow from a piece of leaf placed in soil. Many plants clone themselves by growing shoot-like structures called **runners**. Small plantlets grow from the runners and these are identical to the parent plant.

Creating Copy Cat

Veterinary surgeons at Texas Veterinary College explained that they produced Copy Cat by taking an egg cell from a donor cat and replacing the egg nucleus, containing the genetic material, with a skin cell nucleus from the 'parent' cat.

They were able to get the egg cell to start dividing as it would if it had been fertilised by giving it a small electric shock. The developing cat embryo was then implanted into a **birth mother** who gave birth to Copy Cat. Copy Cat was a genetic copy of her

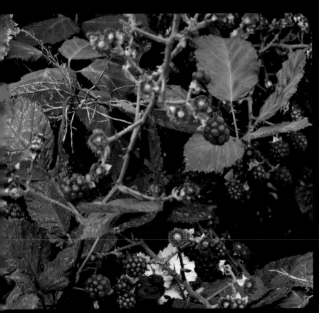

▲ Identical blackberry plants grow from runners

B How might cloning prevent an endangered animal from becoming extinct? (Level 5)

C Scientists involved in cloning Copy Cat were funded by a businessman. He wants to charge wealthy pet owners to clone their animals. (i) Discuss why the businessman was happy to pay for the research. (ii) In your opinion is this type of funding ethical? (Level 6)

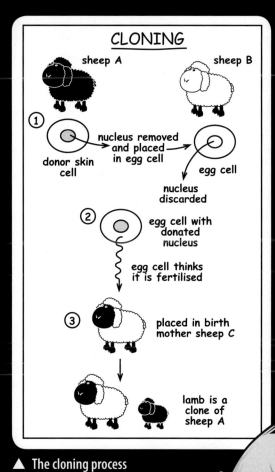

▲ The cloning process

CLONING

sheep A   sheep B

① donor skin cell — nucleus removed and placed in egg cell → egg cell — nucleus discarded

② egg cell with donated nucleus — egg cell thinks it is fertilised

③ placed in birth mother sheep C

lamb is a clone of sheep A

Science to the rescue

Some scientists think that cloning might help save rare breeds like the White Rhino. Humans could eventually live in a world where there is no extinction.

I don't understand why scientists are not allowed to clone humans. Lots of other animals have been successfully cloned such as horses, sheep, dogs and cats.

Cloning research

The Human Fertilisation and Embryology Authority (HFEA) was set up to consider and control what scientists can do in the area of human cloning. At the moment it is illegal in the UK to use cloning in an attempt to create a human. Scientists at Newcastle University have been granted a licence to use cloning to research new treatments for diabetes.

I don't agree with you. Dolly, the cloned sheep, had to be put to sleep because she had arthritis. You wouldn't do that to a human!

D Suggest five questions that you would like to ask a scientist about human cloning in order to understand how and why it might be carried out. (Level 7)

E Mrs Aziz tells her pupils, 'Although clones are genetically identical, cloned animals will never be completely identical to the donor'. Explain what she means and give reasons for your answer. (Level 8)

Keywords
birth mother, clone, donor mother, runner

Assess your progress

2.2

1 Yeast is a fungus made up of single cells and reproduces by asexual reproduction. What do scientists mean by asexual reproduction? (Level 4)

2 Some bacteria are responsible for food poisoning. Explain how a colony of bacteria can increase in size from a small number of individuals to many millions in several hours. (Level 5)

3 Explain the differences between sexual and asexual reproduction, making it clear in your explanation why in asexual reproduction there is only one parent while two are needed for sexual reproduction. (Level 6)

4 Scientists have found fossils of a type of fungus from 460 million years ago which is identical to a modern fungus. This species of fungus reproduces asexually. Suggest how this species has remained unchanged for such a long period of time. (Level 7)

5 Some organisms can reproduce both sexually and asexually. Professor Genius tells his students, 'When environmental conditions are favourable, organisms will use asexual reproduction to make the most of conditions such as abundant food supply, adequate shelter, favourable climate, good light levels etc.'
a Explain what effect this will have on a population.
b Discuss the advantages and disadvantages associated with asexual reproduction. (Level 8)

2.3

1 Tina and Ruth are identical twins. They are the same height but Ruth is much heavier than her sister. What might have caused this difference between the twins? (Level 4)

2 Look at the family tree for the Jones family.

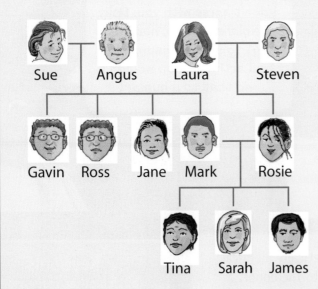

Which two people has Sarah inherited blonde hair from? (Level 5)

3 Gavin and Ross are identical twins. They both have red hair.
a What other two features will they have in common?
b Gavin weighs 55 kg and Ross weighs 63 kg. Suggest reasons why their weights are not the same. (Level 6)

4 a Explain how twin studies are able to shed light on what influences features.
b About 0.2% of the World's population are identical twins. How might this affect a scientist's ability to investigate the effect of the environment on features? (Level 7)

5 One hundred and fifty years ago Sir Francis Galton, who was a cousin of Charles Darwin and a pioneer of twin studies, described twins as 'a living laboratory'. Explain what he meant by this. (Level 8)

2.4

1 What do psychologists study? (Level 4)

2 What do psychologists mean by 'nature' and 'nurture'? (Level 5)

3 Most scientists agree that the environment affects human behaviour in some ways. What does 'environment' mean for a human? (Level 6)

4 a Why are humans very difficult to study?
  b What must psychologists try to do when they design investigations to study human behaviour? (Level 7)

5 a How might hidden cameras help scientists study human behaviour when carrying out an investigation?
  b Do you think it is ethical to study human subjects without their knowledge? Explain your answer. (Level 8)

2.5

1 What are the advantages of selectively breeding chickens that are good egg producers? (Level 4)

2 Thomas's cat has had a litter of six kittens. Five of the new arrivals are normal size for their age but one is very much larger. Discuss the possible reasons for this. (Level 5)

3 Belgian Blue cattle can have problems giving birth to their calves.
  a Describe the features which have been bred into the Belgian Blue cattle.
  b Suggest why their calves often have to be born by caesarean.
  c Write a few sentences to explain whether or not you approve of selectively breeding Belgian Blues with extra muscle genes. (Level 6)

4 The table on the right shows the statistics for cows bred from General and Royal, two different bulls.

Feature	Yield compared with the average	
	Bred from General	Bred from Royal
milk	+900 kg	+1180 kg
fat	+21.7 kg	+32.5 kg
protein	+28.9 kg	+30.8 kg
milking speed	average	fast
temperament	very good	good

a Which bull passed on the genes for the highest milk yield?
b Which bull would you use if you wanted to produce a cow whose milk is to be used to make low-fat yogurt?
c Explain why it is an advantage to the farmer to have cows with good temperaments. (Level 7)

5 General is a bull with a very placid nature. He is easy to handle. Royal is not as gentle. The farmer who owns Royal would like to breed from him because his offspring are such good milk producers but he would like to produce much more manageable animals. Imagine that you are a veterinary surgeon, expert in breeding bulls. Advise the farmer on how he should go about breeding from Royal to produce a good-natured bull. (Level 8)

Assess your progress

2.6

1 Suggest some useful features that might be bred into GM crops. (Level 4)

2 Genetic modification of salmon has produced a fish which grows much quicker than non-modified salmon and needs much less food to grow to the same size. What are the advantages of farming GM salmon? (Level 5)

3 An article suggests that the gene for weedkiller resistance could be transferred accidentally into common weeds causing them to become 'super weeds'.
   a Explain why scientists might want to produce weedkiller-resistant crops.
   b What does the writer of the article mean by 'super weeds'? (Level 6)

4 Genetically modified salmon are farmed in enormous tanks which do not give them access to rivers. The tanks are kept clean and the conditions are just right for the fish to live. They remain in the tanks until they reach the size at which they can be killed for food.
   a Why are GM salmon farmed in tanks rather than in lakes or rivers?
   b Do you consider there are animal welfare issues associated with salmon farming? (Level 7)

5 Explain the ethical issues associated with creating a super athlete. (Level 8)

2.7

1 Make a list of the animal species you know of that have been cloned. (Level 4)

2 Why do gardeners take cuttings of some plants? Explain how they might do this. (Level 5)

3 A farmer has planted an orchard of cloned fruit trees. She says that the orchard will be much easier to manage because the trees are clones. Explain why this is the case. (Level 6)

4 Scientists involved in cloning Copy Cat have said that the technique might be of use in finding a cure for HIV because cats have a form of the disease. Explain how cloning a cat might help human AIDS research. (Level 7)

5 Becca's mother was given a beautiful plant. She looks after it well but it does not produce any flowers so she has no seeds to grow another one. Becca thinks she might be able to produce another plant.
   a Explain with the aid of diagrams how she might be able to do this.
   b Make a list of the features which her mother might want to reproduce in the new plant and explain why the new plant is likely to have these features.
   c Discuss whether plants grown from seeds would also have these features. (Level 8)

3.1 Painting for your life

The Forth Road Bridge in Scotland is over a mile long. Long road and rail bridges, like this one, need to be strong so they are often made of steel which is an alloy of iron. But there is a problem – water and oxygen in the air react with iron. The iron particles join with water and oxygen molecules to form a new substance called hydrated iron oxide. This is the scientific name for rust. If nothing is done to stop a bridge rusting, one day it will collapse. Cars and lorries will plunge into the water below, drowning drivers and passengers.

To stop the Forth Road Bridge from rusting, it is painted. Painting the underside of the steel deck takes about ten years, but the paint used lasts for about 25 years.

Now try these

- Painting iron stops it from rusting. How do you think it does this?

- Iron rusts, making it look dull and brown. Chromium stays bright and shiny. Suggest why chromium doesn't rust.

- Painting iron isn't the only way to stop it from rusting. Can you think of another way?

Coming up in this Chapter ...

Gold is a very unreactive metal – it stays shiny for years

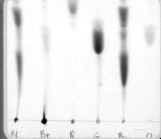

Particles in mixtures can be separated

Aluminium does not rust which make it useful for greenhouses

Some elements are more reactive than others

Learn about:

- what happens to particles during a chemical reaction
- how scientists use models to predict what happens in a chemical reaction
- constructing balanced chemical equations

▲ The University of Birmingham has the first hydrogen filling station

Will you one day fill up the fuel tank of your car with hydrogen? Researchers at the University of Birmingham are trying out the first fleet of hydrogen-powered cars. At the moment cars burn fossil fuels that cause pollution and are non-renewable. Scientists around the world are working hard to find non-polluting, renewable fuels for the cars of the future.

Newsflash

If hydrogen powered cars become the transport of tomorrow, a whole new system of filling stations will need to be built – this will cost a lot of money.

A Give one advantage and one disadvantage of using hydrogen to power cars. (Level 4)

A cleaner fuel?

Fossil fuels, such as petrol, contain compounds called **hydrocarbons**. These contain hydrogen and carbon atoms only. When hydrocarbons are burned, they produce carbon dioxide and water. Most scientists think that too much carbon dioxide in the atmosphere is causing global warming. One example of a hydrocarbon is **methane**. The word equation for the reaction of methane with oxygen is:

methane + oxygen ⟶ carbon dioxide + water

When hydrogen burns the only product is water:

hydrogen + oxygen ⟶ water

B Why do scientists think that hydrogen will be a 'cleaner' fuel than petrol? (Level 5)

What goes in must come out

Look at the particle model on the left showing the reaction of methane with oxygen.

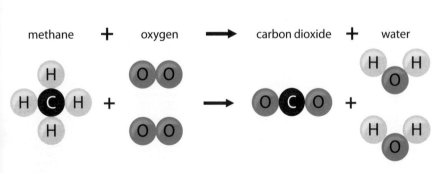

methane + oxygen ⟶ carbon dioxide + water

C Count the number of each type of atom on each side of the arrow – what do you notice? (Level 6)

You have already learned that the mass of the products of a reaction is equal to the mass of the reactants – this is called the **conservation of matter**. We can explain this using the particle model – the particles in the reactants are simply rearranged to make the products. There is the same number of atoms in the reactants as there is in the products. This can help scientists to predict what will happen in a chemical reaction.

> Scientists use symbols to represent atoms because it is much quicker than writing the whole word.

A balancing act

You now know that the atoms that go into a reaction as reactants must come out at the other side as products. You can use this idea to write balanced **symbol equations**.

The molecule hydrogen can be written as H_2 – the small '2' shows that it has two hydrogen atoms. In the same way, oxygen can be written as O_2. Water contains two hydrogen atoms and one oxygen atom, so it is written as H_2O. H_2, O_2 and H_2O are called **chemical formulae**.

D One molecule of hydrogen (H_2) reacts with one molecule of chlorine (Cl_2). How many molecules of hydrogen chloride (HCl) are formed? (Level 7)

Writing balanced symbol equations

The diagrams show how we can write the symbol equation for the reaction between hydrogen and oxygen:

Step 1 – Write down the reactants and the products in an equation

hydrogen **+** oxygen ⟶ water

H_2 **+** O_2 ⟶ H_2O ✗

There's something wrong with this equation – there are two oxygen atoms on the left but only one on the right. If you write a '2' in front of H_2O, the number of oxygen atoms on the left and right are equal:

Step 2 – Balance the number of oxygen atoms

H_2 **+** O_2 ⟶ $2H_2O$ ✗

But now there are four hydrogen atoms on the right but only two on the left. You can fix this easily by adding a 2 in front of the H_2:

Step 3 – Balance the number of hydrogen atoms

$2H_2$ **+** O_2 ⟶ $2H_2O$ ✓

There are now four hydrogen atoms and two oxygen atoms on the left, and four hydrogen atoms and two oxygen atoms on the right – this is a **balanced equation**.

E Now try to balance the equation for the reaction of sodium with chlorine: $\_Na + Cl_2 \rightarrow \_NaCl$. (Level 8)

Keywords
balanced equation, chemical formula, conservation of matter, hydrocarbon, methane, symbol equation

Learn about:

- how to plan an investigation to test a claim
- how different substances react at different speeds
- how metals, metal oxides and metal hydroxides react with acids

▶ The makers of NO-RUST claim iron need only be painted once and will never rust

NO-RUST

5 YEAR GUARANTEE

RUST FREE
RUST PROOFING
NO-RUST
PAINT
5 YR GUARANTEE

ONCE IRON OR STEEL IS PAINTED WITH **"NO-RUST"** PAINT, IT WILL NEVER RUST OR NEED PAINTING AGAIN !

A What's wrong with the claim that once you've used NO-RUST the iron will 'never' rust? (Level 4)

Does NO-RUST work?

Class 9c decide to test how good NO-RUST really is. While they are planning their experiment they make some notes about what they should do.

B How will using several pieces of iron improve this investigation? (Level 5)

- Paint a piece of iron with NO-RUST and put it in water to see if it rusts.
- Put a piece of iron that has not been painted into water as a **control**.
- Use the same source of water at the same temperature for the painted iron and the iron that is not painted.
- Leave all of the samples in water for the same length of time.
- Use several pieces of painted iron and several pieces of iron that have not been painted, instead of just one of each.

Class 9c set up their experiment and leave it for 7 days. They find that iron painted with NO-RUST does not rust, but iron that is not painted does rust.

Iron rusts when it reacts with water and oxygen. The paint stops water and oxygen from reaching the iron.

Does aluminium rust?

Class 9c try leaving pieces of aluminium in water for 7 days. These do not rust. They find this surprising because aluminium is a more **reactive** metal than iron. The aluminium does in fact react with oxygen, and a thin layer of aluminium oxide is formed on the surface of the metal. This layer acts as a barrier that stops more oxygen (and water) from reaching the aluminium underneath. When iron rusts, a layer of iron oxide is formed on the surface but iron oxide is not waterproof so this layer doesn't stop the metal from continuing to rust.

C Even though aluminium is more reactive than iron, it doesn't seem to rust. Explain why this is. (Level 6)

Reacting with oxygen

Many substances react with oxygen. Some react slowly, such as iron rusting. Copper reacts even more slowly with oxygen than iron does. Magnesium reacts very quickly with oxygen – a piece of magnesium can react completely in a few seconds.

When iron rusts, it reacts with oxygen in a very unusual way. First it reacts with the water to give iron hydroxide. Iron hydroxide is a type of **metal hydroxide**.

iron + water ⟶ iron hydroxide

Then the iron hydroxide reacts with oxygen to form hydrated iron oxide – this is the scientific name for rust. Rust is a type of **metal oxide**.

iron hydroxide + oxygen ⟶ hydrated iron oxide (rust)

Acid attack!

Metals react with acids to form **salts** and hydrogen gas.

metal + acid ⟶ salt + hydrogen

Salts are a special type of compound. The name of the salt formed comes from both the name of the metal and the acid.

- Sulfuric acid forms sulfates.
- Hydrochloric acid forms chlorides.
- Nitric acid forms nitrates.

For example:

zinc + sulfuric acid ⟶ zinc sulfate + hydrogen

Rust removers

You can remove the layer of rust from a metal using a rust remover. Rust removers contain an acid and they work because metal oxides react with acids:

iron oxide + phosphoric acid ⟶ iron phosphate + water

Unlike the rust, the iron phosphate formed can be easily scrubbed off, leaving the good metal below.

Metal oxides and metal hydroxides react with acids in the same way – they give a salt and water:

metal oxide + acid ⟶ salt + water

metal hydroxide + acid ⟶ salt + water

E What is the name of the salt formed when calcium hydroxide reacts with nitric acid? (Level 8)

▲ Magnesium reacts very quickly with oxygen

D What is the name of the salt formed when magnesium reacts with hydrochloric acid? (Level 7)

Interesting fact

Cola soft drinks can be used to remove rust. Cola contains phosphoric acid that reacts with the rust to form a soluble salt which can easily be washed off.

Keywords
control, metal hydroxide, metal oxide, reactive, rust, salt

Learn about:
- how zinc can be used to stop iron from rusting
- what displacement reactions are and how they are used

▲ When steel is coated with a layer of zinc this is called galvanising

As you speed along a motorway, you probably do not pay much attention to the metal barrier between the carriageways. It is made of steel, but this is covered with a thin layer of zinc. The zinc layer stops the iron in the steel from rusting. The process of covering steel with a layer of zinc is called **galvanising**.

A Why is it important that motorway barriers do not rust? (Level 4)

Protecting steel

Steel that is painted will rust if the paint is scratched. Galvanised steel does not rust, even if the layer of zinc is scratched exposing the steel underneath. The zinc reacts with oxygen to form zinc oxide – it corrodes in place of the iron because zinc is more reactive than iron. The zinc 'sacrifices' itself to protect the iron, so scientists call this **sacrificial corrosion**.

B How does zinc protect steel from rusting? (Level 5)

Swapping places

A more reactive metal can take the place of a less reactive metal in a compound. Aluminium is more reactive than iron so can displace the iron from iron oxide:

aluminium + iron oxide → iron + aluminium oxide

This is called a **displacement reaction**.

When aluminium displaces iron from iron oxide, the reaction gives out lots of heat. Scientists say that the reaction is highly **exothermic**. The reaction takes place at such a high temperature that the displaced iron is molten. The reaction is used to weld together the rails on a railway track and is called a **thermite reaction**.

▲ You can think of this reaction in terms of oxygen changing its partner – it prefers the aluminium to the iron

C Why is it useful that this displacement reaction is highly exothermic? (Level 6)

Getting the metal

Displacement reactions can be used to extract some metals from their **ores**.

Titanium is a very strong metal that does not corrode easily. It is used to make artificial joints, parts for aircraft engines and pipes in nuclear power stations.

D Explain why titanium is used to make artificial joints. (Level 7)

Titanium is obtained from its ore, rutile, which contains titanium oxide. The process used to extract titanium from rutile was invented by William Kroll in Luxembourg in 1938. During the 1940s, Kroll moved to the United States and developed this process to work on an industrial scale – at that time, due to World War II, there was a need for stronger, lighter metals. The Kroll process is still used today to obtain titanium metal – the titanium oxide is first made into titanium chloride and then magnesium is used to displace the titanium metal:

magnesium + titanium chloride $\rightarrow$ magnesium chloride + titanium

Because magnesium is more reactive than titanium, it swaps places with it.

E Titanium chloride has the formula $TiCl_4$. Balance this symbol equation for the displacement of titanium from titanium chloride by magnesium: $\_\_Mg + TiCl_4 \rightarrow \_\_MgCl_2 + Ti$ (Level 8)

William Kroll's process replaced a previous method invented by Matthew Hunter in 1910. The Hunter process uses sodium to displace the titanium. The Kroll process is cheaper and has led to a more wide-scale use of titanium.

Using models

You can think of a displacement reaction in terms of the substances changing partners, but scientists use the particle model.

You know that a metal will react with an acid to give a salt and hydrogen. This is actually a displacement reaction. For example, when magnesium reacts with hydrochloric acid the magnesium displaces the hydrogen:

$$Mg + 2HCl \rightarrow MgCl_2 + H_2$$

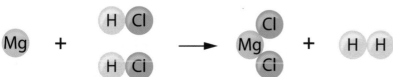

Magnesium atoms (Mg) take the place of the hydrogen (H) atoms in hydrochloric acid. Hydrogen is displaced and magnesium chloride formed.

▲ The molten iron that is displaced from iron oxide during the thermite reaction runs into the gap between the rails. When it solidifies it holds the rails together

▲ An artificial hip made from titanium

Science to the rescue

A mixture of titanium and nickel is used to make 'memory metal'. When bent it returns to its original shape. One use is for glasses frames, which will not break even if you sit on them!

Keywords

displacement reaction, exothermic, galvanising, ore, sacrificial corrosion, thermite reaction

3.5 All that glitters

Learn about:

- how the reactivity of a metal determines its possible uses
- how to place metals in order of reactivity
- how scientists use the reactivity series to predict reactions

▶ Jewellery is often made from gold

You already know that it is important to use the right metal for a job. Each metal has different properties that are suitable for different uses. Jewellery is often made from gold because this is a very **unreactive** metal. It will not react with other substances, and so does not lose its attractive appearance.

Copper is a fairly unreactive metal. It is used for water pipes in houses because it does not corrode.

A Suggest why iron is not used for water pipes. (Level 4)

Reaction of metals with water and acid

Class 9c watch a demonstration given by their science teacher. The teacher shows them how different metals react with water and with dilute acid.

- When metals react with water, a metal hydroxide and hydrogen are formed.
- When metals react with acids a salt and hydrogen gas are formed.

They watch what happens when the teacher adds a small piece of each metal to cold water, and note down how fast each of the metals is reacting.

They use these observations to put the metals in a table with the most reactive at the top. This is called a **reactivity series**.

Reactivity series of metals

Metal	Reaction with cold water	Reaction with dilute acid	
potassium	reacts explosively	reacts explosively	most reactive
sodium	reacts violently	reacts explosively	
calcium	reacts quickly	reacts very quickly	
magnesium	reacts slowly	reacts quickly	
aluminium	reacts very slowly	reacts steadily	
zinc	no reaction	reacts slowly	
iron	no reaction	reacts very slowly	
lead	no reaction	almost no reaction	
copper	no reaction	no reaction	least reactive

Displacement reactions of some metals

Metal	Solution			
	magnesium chloride	zinc chloride	lead chloride	copper sulfate
magnesium	no reaction	grey zinc formed	grey lead formed	brown copper formed
zinc	no reaction	no reaction	grey lead formed	brown copper formed
lead	no reaction	no reaction	no reaction	brown copper formed
copper	no reaction	no reaction	no reaction	no reaction

Displacement reactions

You have already learned that a more reactive metal can displace a less reactive metal from a compound. Displacement reactions can be used to place metals in order of reactivity.

An experiment is carried out to investigate the reactivity of magnesium, zinc, copper and lead. A piece of each metal is placed into a solution of a salt of each of the other metals. A displacement reaction will take place if the first metal is more reactive than the metal in the salt in the solution. The table shows whether a reaction took place, and if so what was formed.

Magnesium displaces all of the other metals. It is the most reactive of these four metals. Copper displaces none of the others, so it is the least reactive.

C Why does zinc displace copper from copper sulfate solution but not displace magnesium from magnesium chloride solution? (Level 6)

D Write a word equation for the reaction when magnesium is added to zinc chloride solution. (Level 7)

Making predictions

The reactivity series of metals can be used by scientists to predict how metals and metal compounds will react.

A more reactive metal will form compounds that are less likely to break down when heated. When sodium carbonate is heated there is no reaction. When calcium carbonate is heated it breaks down into calcium oxide and carbon dioxide.

E Looking at the reactivity series, what would you expect to happen when magnesium carbonate is heated? (Level 8)

B How does the table show that copper is less reactive than iron? (Level 5)

Science to the rescue

Many years ago, lead was used for house water pipes instead of copper. The lead in these pipes can form poisonous lead compounds in the water. It has been illegal to install lead pipes in new houses since 1969.

Keywords
reactivity series, unreactive

49

3.6 Murder in the lab

Learn about:

- how substances can be separated
- how forensic scientists can use information from separation techniques
- how forensic scientists work safely

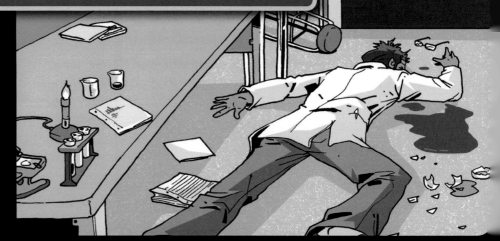

▲ Who killed Mr Jones?

Mr Jones, a science teacher, is found lying dead in a pool of blood on the laboratory floor. Police find brown fibres on his white lab coat. These are sent to a **forensic science** laboratory for analysis. The police arrest the school caretaker, Mr Broom, who is wearing a brown jumper. They also send his jumper for analysis.

A Why do the police send the brown fibres from Mr Jones' lab coat and Mr Broom's jumper to the forensic science laboratory? (Level 4)

Chromatography

Forensic scientist Dr White compares the dyes in the fibres found on Mr Jones' lab coat with those in the fibres of Mr Broom's jumper. He uses a technique called **chromatography**.

Spots of different dyes are placed on paper. The bottom of the paper is then placed in a **solvent**. The solvent rises up the paper carrying the dyes with it. Different dyes are separated as they are carried different distances up the paper.

If spots of brown dye from the two fibres separate into the same colours, which then travel the same distances up the paper, they must both be the same dye.

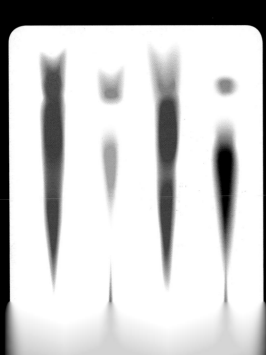

B Explain how Dr White will know if the fibres found on Mr Jones' body are likely to be from Mr Broom's jumper. (Level 5)

This page from Dr White's lab book shows chromatographs of the dyes from the fibres found on Mr Jones' lab coat and from Mr Broom's jumper.

> **C** (i) What do the chromatographs show? Explain your answer. (ii) Does this evidence suggest that Mr Broom is the murderer? (Level 6)

Physical and chemical properties

The particles in different substances often have different chemical and physical properties. Scientists can use these properties to separate the different particles. Particles may be different sizes, have different forces of attraction between them, causing the substances to have different melting points and boiling points, or have different **solubility** in water and other solvents. Because they have different properties the particles behave differently.

In chromatography, the more soluble the particles in a substance are the further they are carried up the paper.

> **D** During paper chromatography, a red dye travels further than a yellow dye. What does this tell you about the properties of these two dyes? (Level 7)

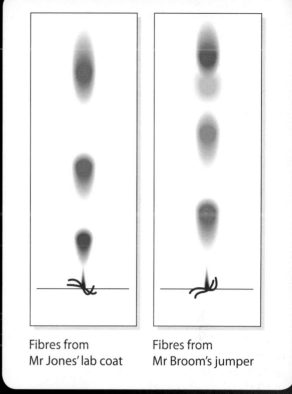

Fibres from Mr Jones' lab coat

Fibres from Mr Broom's jumper

▲ Page from Dr White's lab book

Health and safety in forensic science

As in any laboratory, forensic scientists need to make sure that everything they do is as safe as possible. Here are just some of the safety precautions a forensic scientist needs to take:

- They wear gloves to prevent skin contact when using corrosive **reagents**.

- Because some reagents are toxic, they make sure these substances do not come in contact with the mouth by not eating in the laboratory.

- They wear eye protection when using solutions that could damage the eyes.

- Some reagents are harmful if their vapour is inhaled. This includes solutions that are sprayed to help the scientists see colourless substances. When they are carrying out this type of work, the scientists must use a fume cupboard.

- Another way to 'see' colourless substances is to use ultraviolet light. Some substances that are colourless under visible light appear coloured under UV light. Forensic scientists must be careful when using UV lamps because UV light can damage eyes.

- Forensic scientists must take great care and wear gloves when handling blood-stained clothing. Blood is a potential source of infections such as hepatitis and HIV (AIDS).

> **E** Forensic scientists usually wear overalls, gloves, hats and masks when working in the laboratory. Suggest a reason, other than safety, why forensic scientists wear these items. (Level 8)

> **Keywords**
> chromatography, forensic science, reagent, solubility, solvent

Assess your progress

3.2

1. What is a hydrocarbon? (Level 4)

2. In a chemical reaction, the reactants contain 12 atoms. How many atoms are there in the products of this reaction? (Level 5)

3. Coal is made mainly of carbon. When coal burns, this carbon reacts with oxygen to make carbon dioxide.
   a Write a word equation for the burning of coal.
   b Draw a diagram to show how the particles in carbon and oxygen are rearranged to make carbon dioxide. (Level 6)

4. Four atoms of sulfur, S, react to make four molecules of sulfur dioxide, SO_2. How many molecules of oxygen, O_2, are involved in this reaction? (Level 7)

5. Petrol is a mixture of hydrocarbons, such as octane which has the chemical formula C_8H_{18}. Hydrogen is a possible fuel of the future. Hydrogen can be made from water using a process called electrolysis. This splits water, H_2O, into the two elements that it is made from.
   a Why is hydrogen a more environmentally friendly fuel than petrol?
   b Balance this symbol equation for the burning of octane: $C_8H_{18} + O_2 \rightarrow CO_2 + H_2O$ (Level 8)

3.3

1. Suggest why water pipes in houses are made from copper and not from iron. (Level 4)

2. Steel is made mostly of iron and so it rusts. A company develops a new additive that can be mixed with molten steel. They claim that this new steel will not rust. A team of scientists decide to test the claim made by the company.
   a Briefly describe how they will carry out this test.
   b The scientists also test ordinary steel without the additive. Suggest why they do this. (Level 5)

3. If you want to compare how much painted iron rusts with iron that is not painted, you need to keep all the other factors that might affect the results the same. List three of these factors. (Level 6)

4. What is the name of the salt formed when potassium hydroxide reacts with sulfuric acid? (Level 7)

5. Some pupils want to make copper nitrate. They decide to use the reaction between an oxide and an acid.
   a What are the names of the oxide and acid the pupils must use?
   b Suggest how can they make sure that all of the acid is used up. (Level 8)

3.4

1 Iron is more reactive than copper. If a piece of iron is added to a solution of copper sulfate the outside of the iron becomes coated with a brown solid. This brown solid is copper. Explain why the brown solid forms on the iron. (Level 4)

2 Steel nails used to fasten garden fences are usually galvanised, but steel nails used inside houses are not. Suggest an explanation for this difference. (Level 5)

3 In the Kroll process, titanium is displaced from titanium chloride by magnesium. Titanium can also be displaced by sodium, but not by gold. Suggest a reason for this. (Level 6)

4 When powdered zinc, Zn, is mixed with a solution of copper sulfate, $CuSO_4$, a displacement reaction takes place. Write word and symbol equations for this displacement reaction. (*Hint:* The chemical formula for zinc sulfate is $ZnSO_4$.) (Level 7)

5 In the extraction of chromium, the metal is displaced from its oxide by aluminium. Complete this symbol equation for the extraction of chromium. (*Hint:* The chemical formula for aluminium oxide is Al_2O_3.) (Level 8)

$Cr_2O_3 +$ _____ Al _____ $+$ _____ Cr

Assess your progress

3.5

1 Zinc displaces iron from a solution of iron sulfate. Aluminium displaces both iron and zinc from their solutions. Place zinc, iron and aluminium in order of reactivity. (Level 4)

2 Table 1 shows a number of metals in order of reactivity and Table 2 shows the dates of their discovery.

Table 1	
potassium	most reactive
sodium	
calcium	
magnesium	
aluminium	
zinc	
iron	
lead	
copper	
silver	least reactive
gold	

Table 2	
gold	ancient
silver	ancient
copper	ancient
lead	ancient
iron	ancient
zinc	1746
potassium	1807
sodium	1807
calcium	1808
magnesium	1808
aluminium	1827

a Look at Tables 1 and 2. Many metals have been used since ancient times. What can be said about the reactivity of these metals?

b Some of the metals shown in Tables 1 and 2 were discovered in the late eighteenth and nineteenth centuries. What can be said about the reactivity of these metals? (Level 5)

3 Cheap, gold jewellery is often made from iron coated with a thin layer of gold. Suggest why iron is OK to use under the gold. (Level 6)

4 Suggest why there is a connection between the reactivity of metals and the date of their discovery. (Level 7)

5 Potassium was discovered in 1807. Caesium was not discovered until 1860.

a What does this suggest about the reactivity of caesium?

b Potassium reacts violently with cold water. Predict what happens if a sample of caesium is added to cold water. (Level 8)

3.6

1   A scientist is using chromatography to test several brands of orange squash. She wants to see if they contain a dye that is banned from use in drinks. The diagram shows the chromatograph that she obtains.

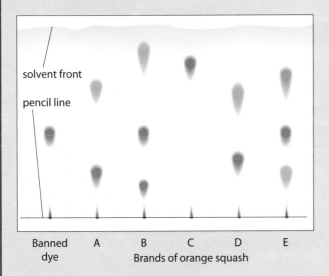

solvent front

pencil line

| Banned | A | B | C | D | E |
| dye | | | | | |

Brands of orange squash

a Which two brands of orange squash contain the banned dye?

b Why did she put all of the dyes on the same piece of chromatography paper, instead of putting each on its own piece of paper? (Level 4)

2   A scientist carries out chromatography to separate different substances that are not coloured. Suggest what he may be able to do to see how far these substances have travelled up the chromatography paper. (Level 5)

3   In chromatography, the place where the spots of coloured mixtures are placed at the start is called the origin. The origin is marked using a pencil. Suggest why this line is not marked with a pen. (Level 6)

4   During paper chromatography, different dyes travel different distances up the paper. Suggest an explanation for why this happens. (Level 7)

5   The most common solvent used for paper chromatography is water. But to separate some mixtures other solvents such as alcohol are used. Suggest why solvents other than water are sometimes used for paper chromatography. (Level 8)

This planet provides the oxygen, water, soil and other resources that we need in order to be able to live. It has a climate that supports a variety of animal and plant life. We need to make sure that the way we live now does not damage the planet so that it cannot provide for us and future generations. We only have one planet. When this one is used up, worn out, overheated or poisoned, what will happen to human life?

Some problems include waste gases produced by burning fuels that contribute to global warming which will lead to climate changes. Waste products from industries and homes need to be disposed of in a way that does not harm soils, water supplies or wildlife.

Scientists are working on short-term and long-term solutions to global warming and waste management. They are finding ways of reducing waste and energy loss. They are also finding ways of making cars and industry greener and cleaner. Everyone needs to find ways of living that are sustainable to make sure that the environment is protected and money is not wasted.

Now try these

- Why might food become more scarce and expensive in the future?

- What evidence is there that the world's climate is changing?

- You've heard the phrase 'reduce, reuse, recycle'. Suggest changes you could make to the way you live.

Coming up in this Chapter ...

Should city dwellers worry about the air they breathe?

Everyone is being encouraged to recycle. How does this improve the environment?

How many people have a supply of safe, clean water?

As the climate changes, habitats change. What is the impact on wildlife?

4.2 Rain pain

Learn about:

- how rain can become polluted
- how rain can transport pollutants into rivers and lakes
- how scientists are dealing with the problems of acid rain

▲ This lake in Canada is one of many affected by acid rain

Canada has many lakes which provide important habitats for fish and water birds. Lakes in Ontario have been badly affected by **acid rain**. The numbers of fish have decreased and the numbers of birds, which rely on fish for food, have also reduced.

Science at work

Canadian lakes are important breeding sites for water birds called loons. Regular monitoring of the loon population tells scientists how well lakes are recovering from acid rain pollution.

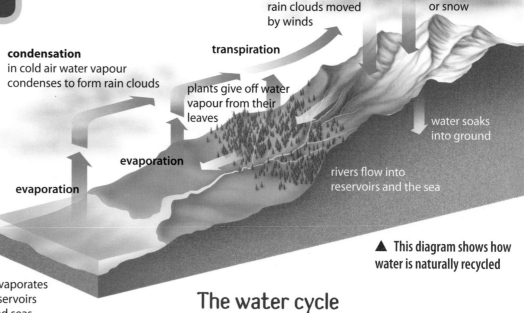

condensation
in cold air water vapour condenses to form rain clouds

precipitation

water falls as rain or snow

rain clouds moved by winds

transpiration

plants give off water vapour from their leaves

water soaks into ground

evaporation

rivers flow into reservoirs and the sea

evaporation

water evaporates from reservoirs lakes and seas

▲ This diagram shows how water is naturally recycled

The water cycle

The diagram above shows the **water cycle**. If **pollutants** enter the water cycle, their effects could be serious.

Gases such as sulfur dioxide are produced when fossil fuels burn. Sulfur dioxide dissolves in rain, turning the water into dilute sulfuric acid. The pH of the rain is lowered from nearly 7, which is neutral, to less than 6.

When acid rain falls it damages plants and plant leaves. It also breaks down the nutrients in the soil that trees and other plants need. When the acid rain drains into the lakes they can become so acidic that plants and animals in the lakes are killed.

> **A** Explain how rain becomes acidic. (Level 4)

Acid lakes

Acid rain can react with metal compounds in rocks and turn them into soluble chemicals that run into the ground and into rivers and lakes. These metal compounds can be more harmful than the rain itself. They can poison plants and animals living in the water. Some plants and water creatures are more sensitive to pH changes than others, so as the pH of the lake changes, so do the species found there.

▲ Acid rain can damage buildings

B The food chain for the lake is: lake plants → water insects → fish → herons. When the lake becomes acidic the plants die off. How will this affect the heron population? (Level 5)

C In the winter, acid rain becomes acid snow. Suggest why the fish population in the lake suddenly drops when the weather warms in spring. (Level 6)

Tackling acid rain

Lime or calcium hydroxide is a **base**. Some dead, acidic lakes have been brought back to life by being 'limed'. Planes and helicopters are used to drop tonnes of lime into the water to neutralise it.

Acid lakes have a low pH of about 5.6. Adding lime raises the pH to 7. This is a very expensive cure for the problem. It is better to tackle the cause and scientists are developing fuels that are less polluting.

D Write the word equation for the neutralisation reaction between calcium hydroxide and sulfuric acid. (Level 7)

E Some lakes have limestone lake beds. Limestone is a base, like lime. Explain how a limestone lake bed prevents the lake water becoming acidic. (Level 8)

Useful bacteria

Bacteria in the sediment at the bottom of some lakes take in the sulfuric acid that has fallen into the lakes as acid rain. They turn it into chemicals called sulfites.

Scientists collect samples of the sediment. They measure the amount of sulfite in the sediment. If it is high, the bacteria are removing acid from the lake. This can help to keep the pH of the lake water close to 7. When a lot of water enters the lake quickly, from heavy rainfalls or snow melts, the bacteria may not be able to remove all the acid.

▲ This lake is in a cold area close to many factories that burn fossil fuels. If it becomes more acidic, some of the lake plants might die

▲ Lime is added to lakes and neutral calcium sulfate is produced

▲ Scientists collect lake water and sediment samples to monitor the health of the lakes

Keywords
acid rain, base, condensation, evaporation, pollutant, precipitation, transpiration, water cycle

4.3 Beware the air!

Learn about:

- how air quality has changed in recent years
- how air pollutants can affect human health
- how scientists study air quality and the types of data that they record

▲ This deadly mixture of smoke and fog covered London in 1952

In December 1952 a mixture of smoke and fog called **smog** blanketed London. Unusual weather conditions trapped a layer of cold, damp air near the ground. Sulfur dioxide produced by burning coal and oil was also trapped and this dissolved into the wet fog. After five days, a breeze took the smog away. But thousands of people died as a result of breathing the acidic, polluted smog.

> **A** Laws were introduced after 1952 to make some areas of London into 'smokeless zones'. What do you think this meant? (Level 4)

▲ The mask filters the air that the commuter breathes

Pollution evolution

Since 1952 the nature of air pollution has changed. Less coal is burned in homes and factories, but industry is still one of the major producers of pollution along with transport. **Ozone** is a reactive gas made of oxygen atoms. Some of the major pollutants found in the air in cities today, and their effects, are given in the table below.

Air pollution			
Pollutant	What it is	Source	Possible effect of exposure to pollutant
nitrogen oxides	gases	reactions in vehicle engines produce fumes containing nitrogen oxides	irritates lungs increases risk of respiratory illness, especially in children
smoke	tiny solid particles	burning fuels, fires and active volcanoes	irritates lungs and makes lung conditions such as asthma worse
ozone	gas	made in the air by a chemical reaction involving nitrogen oxides and using sunlight for energy	irritates lungs and makes lung conditions such as asthma worse
sulfur dioxide	gas	sulfur in fuels such as coal, oil and petrol released by active volcanoes	irritates lungs increases risk of respiratory illness, especially in children

B Oil, coal and petrol all contain sulfur as an impurity. Burning them produces sulfur dioxide. (i) Which is the gas in air that reacts with sulfur when it burns? (ii) Write a word equation for this reaction. (Level 5)

You can use the websites to check air quality in your area

C Wearing a face mask will only protect you from one of the pollutants in the city air. (i) Which one is it? (ii) Why doesn't the mask filter out the other pollutants? (Level 6)

Assessing the danger

Governments have set themselves challenging goals for reducing air pollution. Sulfur dioxide levels are not rising but nitrogen oxide, smoke and ozone levels are. Scientists monitor air quality all over the UK and daily updates on air quality are available on the web.

When the Buncefield oil depot caught fire in December 2005, air quality monitoring stations provided important information about the environmental impact.

A large number of different organisations collected data about pollutants in the air then sent copies of their information to the government website. This is an example of **collaboration**.

Evidence showed that, although the fire was large, air quality in England was not affected.

▲ The smoke from the Buncefield fire could be seen for miles

D Nitrogen dioxide and ozone pollution levels are linked. Ozone levels are high near busy roads on sunny days. Explain why. (Level 7)

E Imagine you have been asked to help the Environment Agency measure the amount of air pollution on your school site. They ask you for advice about the best place to put two detectors: one for measuring smoke and one for measuring ozone. Where would you suggest putting them and why? (Level 8)

Interesting fact

In Victorian times people believed the sea air was full of health-giving ozone. Children with respiratory problems were sent to the seaside for ozone cures.

Keywords
collaboration, ozone, smog

Learn about:

- how carbon dioxide is recycled in nature
- how carbon dioxide emissions can be reduced
- new kinds of fuels
- the impact of choosing a fuel

What is the link between the three photos? The answer is carbon dioxide gas. Plants use carbon dioxide to make food, drinks manufacturers use it to add fizz, and cars on the school run put carbon dioxide into the atmosphere. The management of carbon dioxide is a global issue. In 1997 world leaders met in Kyoto, Japan to agree targets for carbon dioxide reduction. These came into force in 2005. It is hoped that reducing carbon dioxide production will slow down **climate change**.

Recycling carbon dioxide

Carbon dioxide is recycled in nature. It is produced during the process of respiration. When you breathe out, waste carbon dioxide enters the air. Plants take in carbon dioxide from the air. They use this in the process of photosynthesis. The diagram shows the **carbon cycle**.

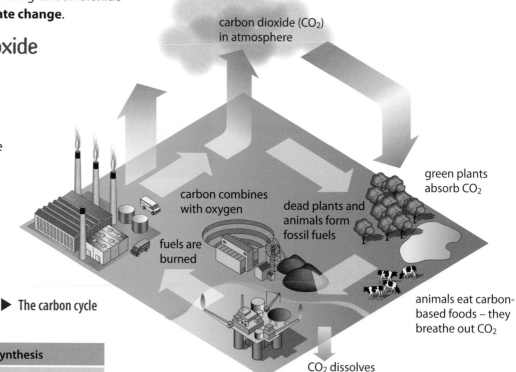

carbon dioxide (CO_2) in atmosphere

green plants absorb CO_2

carbon combines with oxygen

dead plants and animals form fossil fuels

fuels are burned

animals eat carbon-based foods – they breathe out CO_2

CO_2 dissolves in water

▶ The carbon cycle

respiration	photosynthesis
glucose + oxygen → carbon dioxide + water	carbon dioxide + water → glucose + oxygen

A What is the food source used by plants? (Level 4)

What's the problem?

Most scientists believe that the amount of carbon dioxide in the atmosphere is increasing. You don't just produce carbon dioxide by breathing – carbon dioxide is produced every time a fossil fuel is burned, for example when fuels are burned in power stations to generate electricity or used in vehicles. The way people live in the West uses lots of fossil fuels. This means that much more carbon dioxide is produced than can be absorbed by plants.

B Suggest how more carbon dioxide could be removed from the atmosphere. (Level 5)

▲ Petrol and diesel contain carbon in compounds. Burning them produces carbon dioxide

Biofuels

Biofuels are fuels made using plants such as maize or sugarcane. The plants are fermented to produce the fuel ethanol which is an alcohol. Growing fields of plants for biofuels takes carbon dioxide out of the air. If the plants remove as much carbon dioxide while they grow as they release back into the atmosphere when they burn, then they are **carbon neutral**.

But the farming of the crops and the processing needed to turn the plants into usable fuel uses energy. This energy comes from burning fossil fuels, so carbon dioxide is produced. As the biofuels don't take in enough carbon dioxide to balance this, they are not carbon neutral.

There are other problems with growing crops for biofuels. When land is being used to grow fuel crops, it is not available for growing food. If a lot of land is given over to growing biofuel crops, then there will be less grain grown. The maize that was sold for food will be sold for fuel. Sometimes, forests are cut down to make more land available for growing biofuel crops. Older, established trees take in more carbon dioxide than young ones.

Science at work

Scientists are trying to produce a genetically modified floppy tree. It will be easier to turn this into biofuel as it will break down and ferment more easily than a tough, rigid one.

C Explain why a crop that is harvested then re-sown each year takes in less carbon dioxide than a forest of the same size that is left to grow. (Level 6)

Hydrogen fuels

Burning any fuel containing carbon will put carbon dioxide back into the environment. The most environmentally friendly fuel at the moment is hydrogen. When this burns, the only product is water. But producing hydrogen is an expensive process that uses energy and produces carbon dioxide.

D If we only burn trees to produce the energy we need, then it will be easier to be 'carbon neutral'. Do you agree with this statement? Explain your answer. (Level 7)

E Hydrogen fuel needs to be stored and transported under pressure as a liquid. Explain why. (Level 8)

Keywords
biofuel, carbon cycle, carbon neutral, climate change

Learn about:

- why scientists think the climate is changing
- the possible impacts of climate change
- monitoring climate change

▶ Scientists think that flash floods in Bangladesh due to heavy monsoon rain may be a result of climate change

When hurricanes hit and there are floods, you may hear scientists discussing whether these problems are due to climate change. But what exactly is climate change and what causes it?

What is causing climate change?

Scientists have predicted that the average global temperature will rise by 1 °C between 1990 and 2025. This warming of the Earth including its land, oceans and atmosphere is called **global warming**.

Most scientists think global warming is related to the increase in **greenhouse gases**, such as carbon dioxide, in the atmosphere. Scientists think it may be causing the Earth's climate to change. The climate is the general pattern of weather.

It is very hard to predict what the effects of this warming will be on climate, but some of the scientific models suggest that extreme weather, such as hurricanes, may become more frequent and violent.

Gases like methane and nitrogen oxides are also greenhouse gases

A How would you describe the climate of the country you are living in? (Level 4)

What could be causing the warming?

You have already seen that carbon dioxide in the atmosphere stops some heat energy escaping from the Earth. The Earth can also be warmed by extra Sun activity. In addition, when there is less dust in the atmosphere, the Earth warms up. This is because more energy from the Sun gets through.

B Explain how volcanic eruptions help to cool the Earth. (*Hint:* think about what happens during a volcanic eruption.) (Level 5)

The impact of global warming

Global warming will melt more of the ice fields at the poles. As they melt and rainfall increases, seawater will get less salty. This could affect the plankton population. Plankton is a producer in a food chain and all the other organisms in that food chain will be affected too.

As climates change, organisms may not be able to live in the same habitats as before. The animals may move. The plants may grow from seed in new areas that were previously too cold for them.

Possible effects of climate change on some important habitats		
Habitat	Important for	Possible effects of climate change
Arctic tundra	nesting and breeding sites for Arctic sea birds; homes and feeding grounds for lemmings	trees and bushes will take over the tundra and birds and animals will move northwards
North Canadian wetlands and ponds	breeding sites of ducks and geese	wetlands will dry as rainfall decreases and food sources for the geese will decrease
mountain glaciers in South America	providing water supplies for villages in spring and summer	glaciers will shrink, water shortages will threaten villages

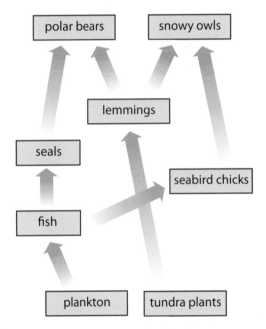

▲ Animals may not be able to adapt quickly enough to cope with climate change.

▲ An Arctic food web

C If climate change causes the polar bear population to decrease through loss of habitat, how will this affect the other organisms in the Arctic food web? (Level 6)

D Explain how a plant species can 'move' from one habitat to another. (Level 7)

E (i) Snowy owls eat seabird chicks and lemmings. Predict how the snowy owl population in the Arctic tundra will be affected by climate change. (ii) The species that live on the tundra at the edge of the ice fields are the most vulnerable to extinction. Explain why. (Level 8)

Science at work

Scientists take samples from the Arctic ice and analyse the air trapped inside. Some of this trapped air has been there for 800 000 years. Studies show that the concentration of carbon dioxide in the atmosphere rose by 31% between 1750 and 2000.

Monitoring climate change

The biggest impact of climate change is seen at the poles. Scientists monitor the Arctic environment. They record changes in animal populations and breeding patterns. They also monitor changes to plant life and habitats.

Keywords
global warming, greenhouse gas

Waste away

▲ Thirty million tonnes of household rubbish are dumped on sites like this each year

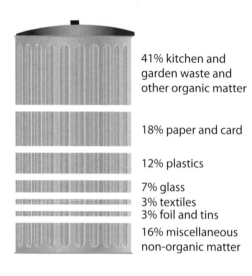

41% kitchen and garden waste and other organic matter

18% paper and card

12% plastics

7% glass
3% textiles
3% foil and tins
16% miscellaneous non-organic matter

▲ The average contents of a dustbin. In the last 10 years, the amount of recyclable material thrown in the bin has reduced

▲ Hospital waste is dangerous. This is why it is burned rather than going to a landfill site

Your rubbish is collected from outside your house. It all goes away, but where does it go? Each person in the UK produces roughly 500 kg of waste each year. About 75% of this ends up in **landfill sites**. These have to be carefully managed to ensure that waste does not contaminate the soils and waterways nearby.

Breaking down waste

Some rubbish such as potato peelings is **biodegradable**. Potato peelings are **organic matter** which means they contain carbon and hydrogen. If peelings are placed in a **compost heap**, they can be broken down by bacteria and other creatures found in soil. The nutrients in the potato can be used as food by the bacteria.

As the potato peelings rot, some nutrients seep into the compost. When the compost is dug into soil, it can provide important nutrients for plants. If the peelings are wrapped in a plastic bag and dumped in a landfill site, their nutritional value is trapped inside the plastic bag and the plastic bag may take hundreds of years to rot. The diagram shows the types of waste that people throw away.

A Look at the dustbin diagram. (i) What percentage of the household waste is biodegradable? (ii) If half the plastics can be recycled, what percentage of all the waste is recyclable? (Level 4)

B Suggest why bacteria are needed for the rotting process. (Level 5)

Up in smoke?

Some industries use burning or **incineration** to get rid of waste materials. Hospital waste such as used scalpels and bandages is often incinerated. Household waste could be incinerated rather than putting it in landfill sites. Burning destroys any harmful bacteria and reduces landfill, but it produces waste gas.

C Organic matter, such as leaves and plant waste, contain carbons and hydrogen. Suggest what is produced when organic matter is burned. (Level 6)

Energy from waste

Plant foods are stores of chemical energy. If you throw them away as waste, you waste that energy. One product of the rotting of organic matter is methane gas. This is produced by the bacteria that are feeding on the waste. Methane gas is an energy source. If biodegradable waste is collected in a **biogas digester** as shown in the diagram, the methane gas produced can be collected and burned, providing useful energy. In India, biogas digesters are used to convert plant waste and manure into methane gas which is then used as fuel.

The engineers building a biogas digester in a village need to work closely with the people there and learn about their lifestyle. Some biogas digester projects have failed because they were either too big for the amount of manure available, or put into areas that were so cold in winter that the bacteria were affected.

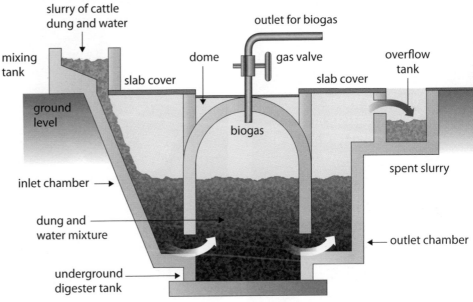

▲ Biogas digesters like this are particularly useful in rural areas

D A biogas digester works best at a temperature of around 35 °C. If the winter temperature falls to 5 °C, what will be the impact on gas production? Explain your answer. (Level 7)

E In villages where biogas has replaced manure as a fuel for cooking in the home, there has often been a reduction in lung and eye problems. Explain why. (Level 8)

Science to the rescue

Scientists have developed biodegradable alternatives to plastic made out of plant starches. These new plastics can be used for carrier bags or for packaging food. They can be composted and broken down by bacteria.

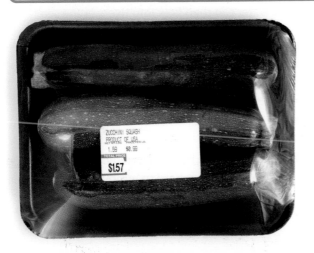

◀ Most plastics are made from fossil fuels. This plastic is made from plant material and is biodegradable

Keywords
biodegradable, biogas digester, compost heap, incineration, landfill site, organic matter

Learn about:

- how waste water is dealt with
- how you get clean drinking water
- how scientists are developing new ways of purifying water

▲ Clean drinking water is very important

▲ In this photo of a sewage treatment plant, you can see the round settlement tanks

▲ Oil and water don't mix and can cause blockages

Would you like a career as a waste water engineer? Spending your days dealing with **sewage** may not sound very glamorous but safe treatment of waste water saves lives. Five thousand children a day die as a result of diseases caused by unclean water.

From loo to river

When you flush water down your loo what happens to it? In the UK waste water is managed by water companies. Drains flow into **sewage works**. The water passes through a series of filters and then enters a **settlement tank** where it stays still for a while so that very fine particles of solid waste that have not been filtered out can sink to the bottom. This is the settling process.

Sometimes chemicals are added to make the very fine particles clump together to speed up the settling process. Bacteria are used to remove the organic matter in the water. When the water is clear, any bacteria or viruses in it can be killed using **ultraviolet (UV) light**. The cleaned water can then flow into rivers or the sea.

> **A** Why does the water pass through filters before it enters the settlement tank? (Level 4)

To pour or not to pour?

Oils and fats don't mix with water. They can form blockages in pipes and at sewage works. Chemicals such as paint and white spirit are hard to remove from the water. Wastes like these should not be poured down the drain. Instead, they should be taken to a recycling centre for disposal.

It's on tap

This diagram shows all the places that water companies take water from. The water goes into a **water treatment works**.

Water that comes from underground has been naturally filtered as it passes through porous rocks. It only needs a little **disinfection** to keep it safe. Reservoir and river water need several stages of treatment. Usually, these will include settlement, filtering and treating with carbon grains to take out any impurities and improve the taste. The carbon grains act like little sponges, absorbing colours and tastes that should not be present. Finally the water can be disinfected using ozone, ultraviolet light or chlorine.

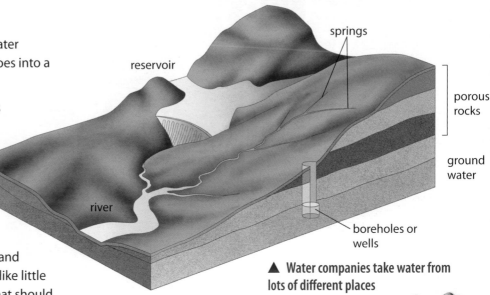

▲ Water companies take water from lots of different places

B What types of impurities will be present untreated in river and reservoir water that will not be found in water from underground sources? (Level 5)

Clean water for all

Scientists are developing new technologies for purifying water. These include tiny chlorine-making products and treating water with small pieces of genetic material that stop fungi breeding.

Foul Fact

In the developing world, one person in ten is infected with an intestinal worm. These have come from contaminated drinking water.

C Suggest why the water needs to be clear before it can be disinfected by ultraviolet light. (Level 6)

Science saving lives

Scientists and engineers are working to provide safe water supplies for villages in developing countries and in disaster areas. They are developing methods for building wells and pumps that work well in the hot climates and use readily available spare parts. Local people are trained to build and maintain their own water treatment works.

▲ One sixth of the World's population does not have access to safe water. These water pumps can save lives

D Water can also be purified by using filters with holes so small that water molecules can pass through but impurities can't. The water needs to be pumped through these filters. Explain why. (Level 7)

E Providing safe water supplies close to each village in a poor region will have a wide range of positive impacts. Suggest what long-term benefits a local well will bring, other than safe water. (Level 8)

Keywords
disinfection, settlement tank, sewage, sewage works, water treatment works, ultraviolet (UV) light

4.8 Use it again

Learn about:
- why metals are recycled
- problems caused by the disposal of metals
- the ethics of recycling

▲ These crushed cans are waiting to be recycled

When you throw something away do you think about whether you could **recycle** it instead? We can get metal ores out of the ground but the supply of metals won't last forever – they are a finite resource. Recycling is a more **sustainable** way of getting metals. It costs money to recycle metals, but it uses less energy and produces less pollution than extracting them from ores.

Today we recycle some metals, but not others. As scientists develop new methods to extract and purify metals from the products that contain them we will be able to recycle more metals.

▲ Recycling cycle

The ores are processed – pure metals are extracted

A mixture of metals go to a recycling plant where they have to be sorted out and melted down

The metal product is bought and used. When the consumer has finished with it they can choose to throw away or recycle

Initially metal ores are mined from rocks. The amount of these ores on Earth is finite and they will eventually run out. The more we mine, the harder it is to find the ore that remains and the more expensive the metals become

Pure metals and metal alloys are used in many manufacturing industries – to make cars, cans, window frames etc

There is always some waste and manufacturers can choose to throw away or recycle

recycle

throw away

Some metals are toxic and the ground becomes contaminated. The land can't be used later and it is expensive to clean up

landfill

throw away

Waste is dumped. Metals corrode slowly and can remain in landfill sites for hundreds of years

A Why do you think the price of some metals is increasing? (Level 4)

B Give two reasons why it is good to recycle metals. (Level 5)

Recycling steel and aluminium

Steel and aluminium are the most commonly recycled metals. Both of these metals are used for making cans. In the UK 12.5 billion steel cans and 37.5 billion aluminium cans are used each year. Many of these are used for soft drinks.

You already know that steel is attracted to a magnet but aluminium is not. **Electromagnets** can be used to separate steel and aluminium in recycling plants. Scrap steel is melted in a furnace with fresh metal to make new steel. This saves iron ore because less new iron is being used to make steel. It also saves energy.

Aluminium is extracted from its ore using a process called **electrolysis**. The ore contains aluminium oxide. Electrolysis uses very large amounts of electrical energy to separate the metal from the oxygen that it is joined to. Electricity is expensive. Recycling uses only 5% of the energy it takes to make new aluminium.

▲ It is easy to send your cans for recycling

> **C** There is plenty of aluminium ore that can easily be mined. But it is still a very good idea to recycle aluminium. Explain why. (Level 6)

Batteries

Nickel and cadmium are two metals that are used to make batteries. Many people use nickel-cadmium rechargeable batteries. Each battery can be recharged up to 1000 times. But eventually even rechargeable batteries cannot be used any more. Both nickel and cadmium are poisonous, and have been linked to cancer. Car batteries contain lead, which is also very poisonous. Other types of batteries contain the metals zinc, mercury and silver.

The average household uses 21 batteries a year. In the UK we throw away about 20 000 tonnes of general purpose batteries every year, but less than 1000 tonnes are recycled. This compares badly with the recycling of small batteries in other European countries. A number of local councils are now running battery collection schemes, but we are still well behind our European neighbours. The bar chart shows how many small batteries were recycled in different countries in 2002.

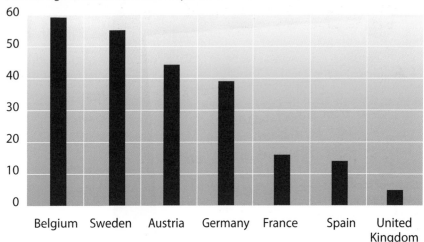

Percentage of small batteries recycled

▲ More batteries are recycled in some countries than in others

> **D** Suggest why more and more nickel-cadmium batteries are being used each year. (Level 7)

> **E** Less than 5% of the batteries used in the UK are recycled. Suggest why. (Level 8)

Ethics of recycling

It is difficult to separate the different metals used in electronic equipment. Many countries export this used equipment to other places for the metals to be separated. Unfortunately in some places not enough attention is paid to the health of workers and the environmental consequences of the methods used. In the future, scientists may develop new methods that will make it possible to carry out recycling of metals from this equipment more easily.

> **Keywords**
> electromagnet, electrolysis, recycle, sustainable

4.9 Detective work

Learn about:

- how environmental scientists monitor pollution
- analysing scientific evidence
- evaluating scientific evidence and working methods

▲ Kingfisher Pool

Field notes

		Water temperature (°C)	River flow rate (m³/s)	pH
Monday	12th	10.04	1.25	6.84
Wednesday	14th	11.17	1.23	6.21
Friday	16th	11.15	1.21	6.35
Sunday	18th	10.34	1.44	6.90
Tuesday	20th	11.20	1.37	6.26
Thursday	22nd	11.09	1.25	6.28
Saturday	24th	10.65	1.23	7.57
Monday	26th	10.08	1.22	6.83
Wednesday	28th	11.11	1.37	6.22

Memo from Project Leader
The report on the unusual pH conditions in Kingfisher Pool is due in 2 days.
Can you let me have your findings?

Thanks

▼ Map of Kingfisher Pool showing surrounding area

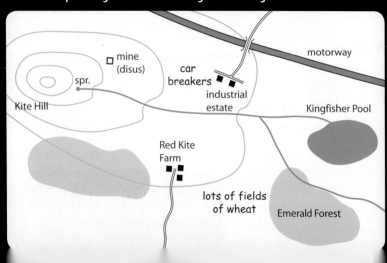

Collecting the data

Here is some information about the testing carried out to investigate the Kingfisher Pool problem.

- flow measurement at mouth of stream
- temperature measurement taken 15 cm below surface of pond using digital temperature probe
- three samples of water taken from pond back to lab in sterilised clean jars for pH testing
- Monday–Friday: temperature readings taken and samples collected at 07.00 h
- Saturday and Sunday: temperature readings taken and samples collected at 09.00 h

A Do you think the pH testing was done using a scientific instrument or indicator paper? Explain your answer. (Level 4)

B The weekday and weekend readings were taken at different times of day. (i) Explain whether you think this matters. (ii) Suggest why the temperature readings were taken 15 cm below the surface. (Level 5)

C (i) What is the range of the pH readings? (ii) Which reading seems anomalous? (Level 6)

D (i) Does the weather record give you enough information to interpret the river flow data? (ii) Does it give you enough information to interpret the water temperature data? Explain your answers. (Level 7)

Weather notes

Mon	Tue	Wed	Thur	Fri	Sat	Sun
12	13	14	15	16	17	18
19	20	21	22	23	24	25
26	27	28				

Field notes

- The soil in the surrounding area is slightly acidic. On Friday 23rd the farmer limed the fields near the stream.

- The car breaker's yard is open from 8.00 am–4.00 pm Monday to Thursday, 8.00 am–2.00 pm Friday.

▲ Lime, a base, is added to an acidic soil to raise its pH

▲ Car batteries contain sulfuric acid

E (i) From all the evidence given, can you suggest why the pH and temperature of the water change as they do? (ii) What further investigation would you need to carry out to test your ideas? (Level 8)

Science at work

In an environmental study like this one, scientists use laboratory instruments to measure levels of oxygen, metals and nitrates from fertilisers in the water.

Assess your progress

4.2

1 Look at the diagram of the water cycle on page 58. What provides the energy for evaporation of water? (Level 4)

2 When water evaporates from muddy puddles, will this water become dirty rain? Explain your answer. (Level 5)

3 a Carbon dioxide, produced by respiration and burning, dissolves in water to make carbonic acid. Explain why rain is always slightly acidic, even in areas where there is very little pollution.

b Rain is officially classed as acid rain when it has a pH of less than 5.6. Why could you not use Universal indicator paper to decide whether or not rain in your area was acidic? (Level 7)

4 Forests that are at high altitude are damaged more by acid rain pollution than those on lower ground. Think about how the weather conditions at the top of a mountain might be different to those in a valley and suggest a reason why high altitude forests are damaged more. (Level 8)

4.3

1 Coal and oil are burned in large quantities in power stations to produce electricity. Reducing your electricity consumption can help improve air quality. List five things you could do to reduce the amount of electricity you use. (Level 4)

2 In December 1991, there was another bad fog in London. People with breathing problems were warned to stay indoors. It lasted 3 days and 160 deaths were thought to have resulted from the pollution. Suggest three reasons why the death rate was far lower during the 1991 fog than the 1952 smog. (Level 5)

3 In December 2005, there was a fire at an oil depot in Buncefield, Hertfordshire, England. At the time, people were very worried about the effects of the smoke plume. Air quality stations in the south of England and in France were monitored for some time afterwards.

a What information would the scientists need in order to be able to track the movement of the smoke plume?

b Why did the scientists collect data from France? (Level 6)

4 Look at the table predicting number of deaths linked to air pollution.

Projected premature annual deaths due to city air pollution

Region	Premature deaths (thousand per year)
Central Europe	20
North-eastern Europe	200
China	590
India	460
Latin America and the Caribbean	130
Sub-Saharan Africa	60

Source: World Bank

a What sorts of information will scientists use to make predictions like this?

b Suggest explanations for the variations in deaths in different areas. (Level 7)

4.4

1 Which of these statements are true about all fuels? (Level 4)

A They are all liquids.

B They all react with oxygen.

C They are all poisonous.

D They all give out energy.

E They are all found underground.

2 All plants contain carbon, stored in sugars and starches. When animals eat plants, some of the carbon can be stored by their bodies. An environmental website claims: 'When you take into account meat's entire lifecycle, each meat eater is responsible for 1.5 more tons of greenhouse gases than a vegan per year'.

a How do animals release carbon back into the atmosphere?

b Suggest why meat production might produce more greenhouse gas than farming grains and vegetables. (Level 6)

3 Look at the newspaper article. Decide whether the statements are true or false, based on the information given. Explain your answers.

A car manufacturer in Japan has started to produce a hydrogen-powered car which does not emit pollution. The car runs on electricity. This electricity is produced by reacting hydrogen with oxygen which produces water. The manufacturer claims that the car is three times more fuel-efficient than a petrol car. Some scientists have pointed out that hydrogen is usually produced from fossil fuels and it is very expensive to produce. An analysis of the effect on the environment of different fuels has shown that, overall, hydrogen cars can produce more carbon dioxide than petrol or diesel cars.

A A hydrogen powered car is powered by electricity.

B Hydrogen powered cars emit as much carbon dioxide as regular cars.

C We won't be able to use hydrogen when fossil fuels run out.

D Hydrogen cars are more efficient so they will be cheaper to run. (Level 8)

4.5

1 Why do you think it would be a problem if the amount of greenhouse gases in the atmosphere reduces too much? (Level 4)

2 Look at the graph showing how carbon dioxide levels have varied over the last 50 years. Why does the line have a zigzag pattern? (Level 5)

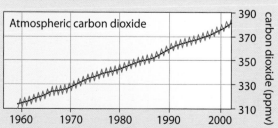

Atmospheric carbon dioxide

(*Hint:* think about processes that add CO_2 to the atmosphere and also ones that remove it.)

3 Look at the information in the table below about some of the factors that affected global temperatures in the twentieth century.

Time period	Level of volcanic activity	Level of solar activity	Level of carbon dioxide production
1910–1945	low	high	high
1946–1976	average	average	high
1976–1999	low	high	very high

Between 1946 and 1976 the rate of global temperature rise slowed. The rate increased towards the end of the century. Use the information in the table to explain this observation. (Level 6)

Assess your progress

4.6

1 This table shows how the amount of rubbish people in the UK recycled changed between 2000 and 2006.

Year	2001	2002	2003	2004	2005	2006
kg per person per year	52	60	71	87	113	135

  a Describe the trend that this data shows.
  b List three types of rubbish that can be recycled. (Level 5)

2 This table shows the mass of rubbish produced by each person in the UK per year.

Year	2001	2002	2003	2004	2005	2006
rubbish recycled (kg per person)	52	60	71	87	113	135
rubbish into landfill (kg per person)	455	456	449	425	404	376

  a Work out the total amount of rubbish produced per person each year. Is there a trend?
  b Estimate the total amount that one person will throw away in 2010.
  c A council sets a target that 30% of waste will be recycled by 2010. Using your answer to b, what mass of recycled rubbish will each person produce each year? (Level 6)

3 Use your knowledge of digestion in the body to explain why biodegradable packaging cannot be used to contain acidic foods. (Level 8)

4.7

1 Water that is filtered through rocks is pure. We can carry out filtration in the lab. Draw a labelled diagram of the apparatus you would use to filter in the science lab. (Level 4)

2 The average person in Britain uses 150 litres of water per day. If water consumption continues to rise at the same rate, we will use 40% more in 20 years. How much water will the average person be using in 20 years time? (Level 5)

3 Water can be purified by boiling it. The boiling point of water is 100 °C. This is only true at standard atmospheric pressure which is 760 mmHg. At lower pressures, water boils at a lower temperature. The table shows how the boiling point of water varies with pressure.

Boiling temperature (°C)	Pressure (mmHg)
101.0	770
97.5	675
93.0	573
88.0	472
79.0	326

  a Increasing the pressure can cause water to boil at above 100 °C. Using the results above, draw a suitable graph to enable you to find out the pressure needed to get water to boil at 105 °C.
  b Air pressure varies with altitude. At an altitude of 1500 m, the atmospheric pressure is 650 mmHg. At what temperature would water boil? (Level 7)

4.8

1 This pie chart shows the different things that people throw away into their dustbins.

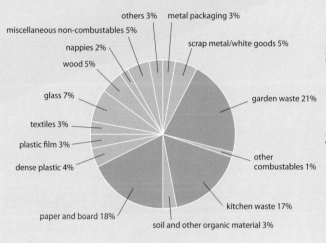

others 3% metal packaging 3%
miscellaneous non-combustables 5%
nappies 2%
scrap metal/white goods 5%
wood 5%
glass 7%
garden waste 21%
textiles 3%
plastic film 3%
other combustables 1%
dense plastic 4%
paper and board 18%
kitchen waste 17%
soil and other organic material 3%

a What percentage of the material thrown away is made of metal?

b Metals are only a small percentage of the total material thrown away. Why is it still important to recycle metals? (Level 4)

2 Cookers, fridges and washing machines are replaced only once in several years. Why is it still important to recycle the metals they are made from? (Level 6)

3 A recycled aluminium can saves enough energy to run a television for 3 hours.

a Explain how this statement is true.

b In the UK about 300 million cans are sent to landfill each year. Approximately how many years could you run a TV for on the energy saved if these cans were recycled? (Level 7)

4 We recycle a lot of steel but very little sodium. Suggest reasons for this difference. (Level 8)

4.9

1 Look at the investigation on page 72. Why did the scientist take three samples of water back to the lab? (Level 4)

2 Would it have been helpful to have known the pH of the rain that fell? Explain your answer. (Level 5)

3 Look at the table of field notes on page 72.

a Draw a graph showing the variation in pH with water temperature. Mark on relevant weather detail.

b Can you draw any conclusions about a link or lack of a link between weather and water temperature? (Level 6)

4 Look at the table of field notes on page 72.

a Draw a graph to show how flow rate, pH and temperatures vary over time.

b Does this graph reveal any patterns?

c Do you have enough data to draw firm conclusions? (Level 8)

5.1 Working under pressure

Imagine what it is like to be an army tank driver. You must be very alert. You must be able to react quickly when under fire and drive the vehicle carefully through muddy fields or shifting sands.

Tanks can weigh up to 69 tonnes, so why do they not get stuck in mud or sand? The answer lies in how their pressure is distributed over the ground. Instead of wheels, tanks have caterpillar tracks.

The gun on top of a tank can move around in a complete circle as well as up and down. This is very important when you are being fired at from all directions. The gun moves using a system called hydraulics. This uses a liquid to transfer pressure from one part of the tank to another.

Now try these

- What do you understand by the word pressure?

- Name the forces acting on the tank as it crosses the field.

- What two factors affect the size of a moment?

Coming up in this Chapter ...

Concorde used to travel at twice the speed of sound. It had to accelerate quickly at take off

Parachute teams need to understand air resistance to put on their displays

Pneumatic tyres make travelling over bumpy ground more comfortable

Some scientists think that levers were used to move the great stones at Stonehenge

Learn about:

- how scientists use graphs to model speed
- what acceleration and deceleration are

Science at work

GATSO speed cameras use radar beams to measure the speeds of vehicles. When a car passes one going too fast, the GATSO takes photographs, using a flash, of the car and its number plate.

▲ Speed cameras calculate the speed of vehicles to catch speeding drivers

The flash from a roadside speed camera is bad news if a driver sees it in their car's rear view mirror. It means that they have been caught speeding and will be fined and get points on their driver's licence.

Speed cameras calculate the speed of a vehicle at a particular point in time. To calculate a car's speed over a whole journey, you can use a **distance–time graph** to model speed.

Dist (m)	Time (s)	Dist (m)	Time (s)	Dist (m)	Time (s)
1089.66	12.12	1089.99	12.23	1089.10	12.04
1089.41	12.32	1089.21	12.23	1089.37	12.54
1089.35	12.44	1089.92	12.23	1089.25	12.18
1089.51	12.23	1089.31	12.61	1089.89	12.95
1089.66	12.12	1089.28	12.23	1089.22	12.67
1089.23	12.15	1089.83	12.84	1089.11	12.11
1089.51	12.17	1089.21	12.63	1089.06	12.92
1089.57	12.12	1089.66	12.53	1089.81	12.01
1089.51	12.42	1089.29	12.23	1089.09	12.54
1089.77	12.78	1089.25	12.11	1089.49	12.56
1089.51	12.54	1089.73	12.24	1089.36	12.99
1089.22	12.12	1089.21	12.63	1089.29	12.50
1089.51	12.11	1089.21	12.23	1089.11	12.02
1089.47	12.19	1089.00	12.44	1089.01	12.54
1089.88	12.12	1089.11	12.81	1089.82	12.88
1089.12	12.10	1089.52	12.23	1089.23	12.39

▲ Some data from a racing car

Distance–time graphs

Bruce is a racing car driver. He needs to know how fast he is going at different places around the racetrack. A lot of data is collected by computers in his racing car. Bruce can compare his data with data collected from other drivers to work out where he is fastest and where other drivers are fastest. The data can be used to produce a distance–time graph. Scientists use graphs to make data easier to understand.

The diagram shows a distance–time graph for one lap of the racing circuit. The slope or **gradient** of a distance–time graph shows the speed. The steeper the gradient, the faster the speed. If an object is not moving, the line on the distance–time graph is horizontal.

A How long does it take to complete the lap? (Level 4)

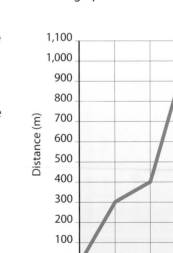

▲ Bruce's distance–time graph

B Look at Bruce's distance–time graph. (i) Between which two times is Bruce's car travelling the fastest? How do you know? (ii) Using the equation 'speed = distance/time', calculate its speed at the fastest point on the graph. (Level 5)

Speed–time graphs

Scientists also use **speed–time graphs** to model speed. The diagram shows a speed–time graph for Bruce's lap on a different circuit.

On a speed–time graph, steady speed is shown by a horizontal line. When Bruce speeds up, the graph's gradient is upwards. Scientists call speeding up **acceleration**. When Bruce slows down, the graph's gradient is downwards. Slowing down is called **deceleration**. You have already seen that objects speed up and slow down because the forces acting on them are unbalanced.

C Look at the speed–time graph. How many times does Bruce accelerate and decelerate on his lap? (Level 6)

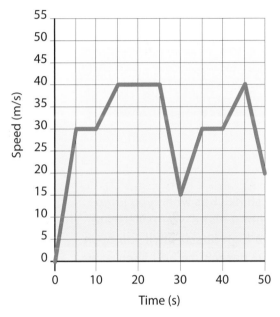

▲ Bruce's lap

The race

Every year in Wales, the Man versus Horse race takes place. In 2004 a human won it for the first time. Sprinters have also raced other animals such as dogs or cheetahs.

Here is some data from a race between a sprinter and a dog. As dogs are usually faster than humans the sprinter is given a head start. What happens is not very clear from the data.

Sprinter v dog race						
Time (s)	0	2	4	6	8	10
Distance (m) (sprinter)	0	20	40	60	80	100
Distance (m) (dog)	0	0	20	50	100	100

D (i) Produce a distance–time graph from the data. (ii) After how many seconds did the dog overtake the man? (iii) How long was the race? (iv) Calculate the average speed of the sprinter. (v) By how many seconds did the dog beat the sprinter? (Level 7)

E (i) What was the dog's speed after 9 seconds? (ii). Calculate the average speed of the dog. (Level 8)

Learn about:

- the forces acting on falling objects
- how speed changes during a parachute jump
- assessing risk

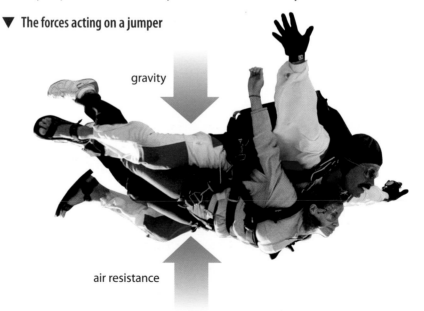

▲ Ready.......steady.......jump

Tony has decided to take part in a parachute jump for charity. He is worried that he will be travelling too fast when he hits the ground. He is very nervous but the instructor tells him it is quite safe and thinks it is safer than skiing.

Falling objects

When objects fall, two different forces act on them. The first force acting on them is weight due to gravity. The second force is **air resistance** or **drag**. This is because when objects fall they are falling through air particles and pushing them out of the way.

The faster an object moves through the air the larger the air resistance. This is just like when you pedal a bike faster, you feel more wind on your face.

▼ The forces acting on a jumper

gravity

air resistance

I think that when you jump from a plane, you accelerate to a high speed until you open your parachute and then stay at the same speed until you hit the ground. Is this right?

Interesting fact

Vesna Vulvovic was a flight attendant who survived falling 10 200 m when her plane blew up in 1972. She remained strapped to her seat and landed in thick snow.

A If the air particles are rubbing against a falling object, what force is acting between them and the object? (Level 4)

Doing the jump

At the start of the jump, Tony's weight is larger than the air resistance. As he falls he accelerates. His weight stays constant, but the air resistance increases. The forces acting on Tony are unbalanced. This causes him to accelerate.

Eventually the air resistance is equal in size with his weight. The forces are balanced and Tony falls at a steady speed. This is called the **maximum speed**.

When Tony opens the parachute, his weight stays the same but the air resistance increases. The forces are unbalanced again and he slows down to a new lower constant speed and is ready to land.

> **B** Look at the diagrams. What else must the two forces be, apart from equal in size, if they are balanced? (Level 5)

> **C** (i) Explain why opening a parachute increases Tony's air resistance. Use the term 'particles' in your answer. (ii) Why does Tony reach a new constant speed after opening the parachute? Think about what will happen to the air resistance as he slows down. (Level 6)

Assessing the risk

Do you think that Tony's instructor was correct when he said that parachute jumping was safer than skiing? The table below shows the number of serious injuries requiring hospital treatment compared with the number of people taking part in an activity. Scientists use data like this to assess how risky an activity is.

Injury data

Activity	Number of injuries	Number of people taking part
skiing	1600	413 200
parachute jump	72	21 150

Unfortunately, for every 50 000 people taking part in parachute jumps, one jumper is killed. The chance of being killed skiing is one for every 1 400 000 skiers. The chances of being injured are reduced by always wearing the correct safety equipment and following the directions of the instructor.

> **D** (i) Calculate the chances of getting seriously injured for both activities. (ii) Would you take part in a charity parachute jump? Explain your answer. (Level 7)

> **E** What information does the injuries data table not give you which might mean Tony's instructor is correct about parachute jumping being safer than skiing? (Level 8)

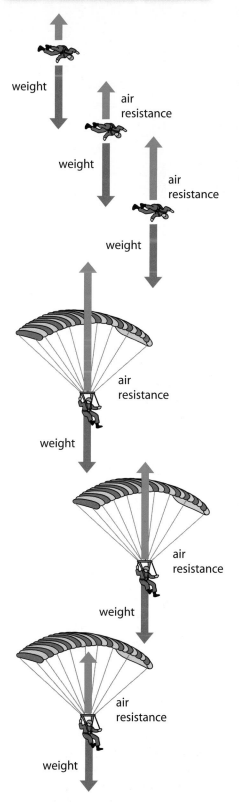

Calculating forces

▲ How the forces acting on a skydiver change during a fall

Keywords
air resistance, drag, maximum speed

5.4 Don't crack the ice

Learn about:

- what is meant by pressure
- the risks involved in driving an ice truck

▲ Driving on a road made of ice

What are the roads like where you live? There are probably a few potholes in some of them. Sometimes these holes are so large people say the road is dangerous. But this danger is nothing compared to driving a truck weighing 60 000 kg on a road made of ice over a frozen lake, as the driver in the photo is doing.

Is it worth the risk?

In winter, it gets so cold in parts of Canada that the lakes freeze over with ice thick enough for a road to be made on them. The ice is only thick enough to support trucks for two months of the year. Dozens of drivers have been killed since the first ice roads were built 50 years ago. Although the job is risky, people still want to do it. Perhaps the thought of earning £45 000 in two months makes them think it is worth it.

A If you were a truck driver would you think about doing the job or is it too risky? Explain your answer. (Level 4)

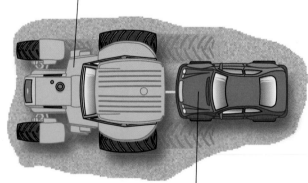

if an object's weight is spread over a large area, then the pressure is low

if its weight is spread over a smaller area, then the pressure is high

Under pressure

The ice will not crack as long as the trucks do not put too much **pressure** on it. You will have already come across the word pressure, but scientists mean something specific when they use it. Pressure tells you how concentrated a force is.

B Look at the photo showing a truck driving on the ice road. How does the truck spread its weight over a large area? (Level 5)

Calculating pressure

Scientists can calculate how much pressure a truck **exerts** on the ice using these equations:

$$\text{pressure (in N/m}^2\text{)} = \text{force (N)/area (m}^2\text{)}$$

or

$$\text{pressure (in N/cm}^2\text{)} = \text{force (N)/area (cm}^2\text{)}$$

If the areas are large, scientists use metres (m^2). If the areas are small they use centimetres (cm^2).

The scientists need to know the weight of the truck and the area of the truck in contact with the ice to work out the pressure.

weight 10 000 N   area of tyres on the ground = 2500 cm^2

weight 15 000 N   area of tyres on the ground = 2000 cm^2

weight 40 000 N   area of tyres on the ground = 10 000 cm^2

▲ Are they safe on the ice?

▲ It's easy to get stuck in muddy fields

C The three trucks in the diagram are travelling over ice that can take a pressure of 5 N/cm^2. (i) Calculate the pressure exerted by each truck. (ii) Which trucks are safe on the ice? (iii) Another truck produces a pressure of 20 N/cm^2 on the ice. If its weight is 15 000 N what area must its tyres have? (Level 6)

Getting a grip

Even off-road vehicles sometimes get stuck in the mud. One way of avoiding this is to let some of the air out of the tyres before driving into a field. The diagram shows what happens to a tyre when you let air out.

D (i) What happens to the area of the tyre on the ground after the air is let out? (ii) Explain why this change reduces the chances of the car becoming stuck. (Level 7)

▲ Letting air out of a tyre can help when you are driving on muddy ground

E The truck in the diagram on the right has a weight of 4000 N. The area of an inflated tyre on the ground is 10 cm^2. (i) Calculate the pressure of the truck on the ground. (*Hint:* remember the number of tyres.) (ii) After the air has been let out, the area of each tyre on the ground is 15 cm^2. By how much has the pressure decreased? (Level 8)

Keywords
exert, pressure

Learn about:

- pressure in liquids
- how car brakes work
- using the particle model to explain hydraulics

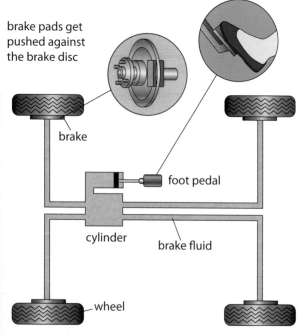

brake pads get pushed against the brake disc

brake

foot pedal

cylinder

brake fluid

wheel

▲ The braking system in a car

▲ Brakes have to work hard in this racing car

A racing car needs to slow down very quickly to get round corners. Cars slow down and stop by using **hydraulics** which is a system that relies on pressure in liquids.

Passing on pressure

When a driver puts their foot on the brake pedal, it puts the liquid in the brake pipe under pressure. This liquid **transmits** the force onto the brakes on each wheel.

The liquid in the brake system cannot be squashed because the particles cannot get any closer to each other. The pressure in a liquid is the same throughout because the force acts equally in all directions. So the force is transmitted from the pedal to the brake pads.

> **A** How does pushing the brake pedal slow down the car? (Level 4)

> **B** Explain in as much detail as you can why using a gas rather than a liquid wouldn't work in a braking system. (*Hint:* think about the particle model.) (Level 5)

Increasing the force

The force you apply to the brake pedal is not enough to slow a car down by itself. The force needs to be magnified. This is done in a hydraulic system by changing the area of the plungers.

The two syringes have different areas and they each have a plunger. You can see in the diagram that if you exert a force of 10 N on plunger A, then plunger B will exert a force of 50 N. The force has been magnified. But how does this work?

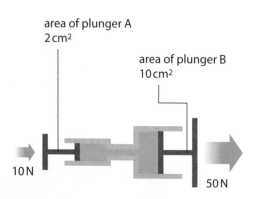

area of plunger A
2 cm²

area of plunger B
10 cm²

10 N

50 N

▲ Increasing the force

Because the pressure on plunger B is the same as the pressure on plunger A, you can work out the force pushing out plunger B using the pressure equation:

$$\text{pressure} = \frac{\text{force}}{\text{area}}$$

pressure on A = force/area
= 10/2
= 5 N/cm^2

force on B = pressure × area
= 5 × 10
= 50 N

Hydraulic machines

In **hydraulic machines**, such as diggers, the liquid-filled syringes are called **cylinders** and the plungers are called **pistons**. When a small force is applied to the small piston, the large piston connected to it exerts a large force.

Hydraulic data collected by an engineer

System	Input force (N)	Input piston area (cm^2)	Pressure (N/cm^2)	Output piston area (cm^2)	Output force (N)
A	5	2.5	?	4	?
B	?	2	10	20	?
C	30	?	3	?	240

C Copy and complete the table above and work out the missing values. (Level 6)

Under pressure

Liquids and gases have their own internal pressure because of their weight. The deeper the water, the higher the pressure. If you swim to the bottom of the deep end of a swimming pool the **water pressure** can hurt your ears.

D Aeroplane cabins have to be pressurised because the air outside is at too low a pressure for people to breathe. Explain why the pressure of the air outside is low. (Level 7)

▲ Hydroelectric dams, such as the Shasta Dam, need very thick walls at the base to withstand the pressure of the water

Science at work

Hydraulics is not only used in machines such as diggers and car brakes. Water pistols also work using hydraulics!

water

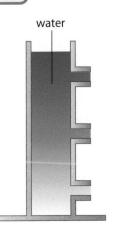

E Look at the diagram of the cylinder of water. (i) Draw a diagram showing the water coming out of the three holes. (ii) Out of which hole will the water coming out travel the greatest horizontal distance? Explain your answer using the word 'pressure'. (Level 8)

Keywords
cylinder, hydraulics, hydraulic machine, piston, transmit, water pressure

5.6 I'm tyred

Learn about:

- how pneumatic tyres were developed
- pressure in gases and what affects it

▶ Riding a bike with wooden tyres isn't very comfortable

John Boyd Dunlop was a Scottish vet living in Belfast in the 1880s. His son complained that when he rode his bicycle to school the cobbled streets made his bottom sore. Dunlop solved the problem by inventing a **pneumatic** tyre. This is a tyre filled with air.

Particles to the rescue

Why does a tyre filled with air make a bike ride more comfortable? You can use the particle model to explain this. Look at the diagrams of the two tyres.

The wood particles in the solid wooden tyre are very close together and cannot be squashed or **compressed**. If you go over a bump all the force transmits to the rider. The air particles in the pneumatic tyre can be compressed because there is space between the particles. This absorbs some of the energy and reduces the shock of going over the bump.

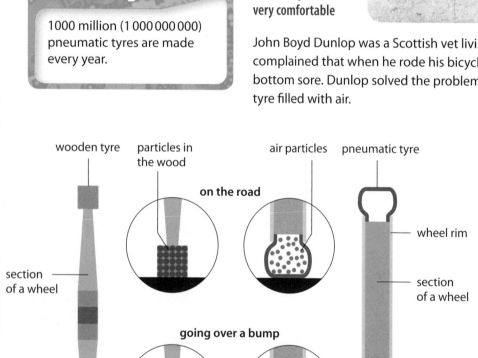

▲ Particles in two different tyres

A Explain using the particle model why the particles of air in a pneumatic tyre can be compressed. (Level 4)

When the air in a tyre gets compressed the particles take up less space, but the number of particles doesn't change. Particles of air inside the tyre are moving around all the time in all directions. The particles of air hit the inside of the tyre and cause the pressure inside it.

B Is the pressure inside a tyre with a slow leak increasing or decreasing? Use the particle model to explain. (Level 5)

> **C** The air in a cylinder is released into another cylinder which has twice the volume. Use the particle model to explain what will happen to the pressure. (Level 6)

> I think if you pump more air into a beach ball there will be less space for the particles to get squashed so it won't bounce as high.

What makes balls bouncy?

> I think if you pump more air into a beach ball it will bounce higher because there are more particles inside.

> **D** Who do you think is correct? Explain your answer. (Level 7)

Amber and Ryan decide to do an experiment. They pump different amounts of air into a beach ball using a bicycle pump and record how high the ball bounces. The table shows their results:

Bouncing ball data									
Number of tyre pumps of air	0	1	2	3	4	5	6	7	8
Bounce height (cm)	0	1	3	6	9	13	20	22	30

> **E** Draw a graph of their results. Use the graph to work out: (i) Whose hypothesis was correct? (ii) Which result is anomalous? (iii) Describe the relationship between the pressure in the ball and bounce height. (Level 8)

The experiment shows that the more often gas particles hit the inside of their container the higher the pressure. So putting more particles inside the ball means that the inside surface is hit more often.

Pressure and temperature

How does temperature affect the pressure of an object? How fast a gas particle moves depends on its temperature. The higher the temperature the faster the particle moves. This means that as the temperature rises, the particles will hit the inside wall of the object more often and harder, so the pressure increases. If you lower the temperature, particles move more slowly and the pressure decreases.

▲ A balloon deflates after it is placed in liquid nitrogen which has a temperature of −150 °C

> **Keywords**
> compressed, pneumatic

Learn about:

- how ancient cultures solved problems
- levers and moments

▶ A shaduf is an ancient device which is still used today to move water

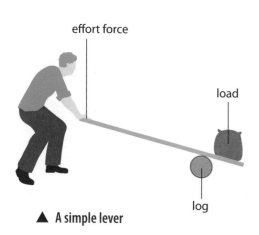

▲ A simple lever

Many thousands of years ago, farmers in ancient Egypt had to get water to their crops. Water pumps had not yet been invented. Instead they used a device called a shaduf to lift water out of the Nile and pour it onto their fields. Water is very heavy and using buckets would be very hard work. Shadufs are so good at moving water they are still used today. They work by using the **principle of moments**.

Levers

You need to understand how machines called **levers** work before you can understand how a shaduf works. A lever is a simple machine that increases the **turning effect** of a force. The turning effect of a force is also called the **moment** of the force.

The plank in the diagram is an example of a lever. The log is the **pivot**. A pivot is the point around which something turns. When the man pushes on the plank it moves around the pivot.

Because the man is further from the pivot than the sack is, he finds moving the sack easier. This is because the size of a moment is increased by increasing the effort force, or increasing the distance the force is applied from the pivot.

Shaduf to the rescue

Look at the diagram of a shaduf and see if you can understand how it works. It is a pole with a large weight at one end and a bucket for the water at the other. The pole rests on a pivot so it can be lifted up and down. The farmer pulls down on the bucket side when it is empty to fill it full of water. Then he lets go and the weight lifts the heavy bucket for him.

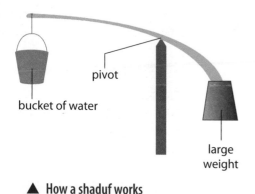

▲ How a shaduf works

A What do you notice about the distance of the weight from the pivot compared to the distance from the bucket to the pivot? (Level 4)

A shaduf is a lever. There are two forces on the beam: the water bucket and the weight. Each of these has a turning effect or moment on the pivot. To calculate the moment you can use the equation:

moment (Nm) = force (N) × distance (m)

B Calculate the moment of the weight and the bucket. (Level 5)

If the bucket was removed, the weight would turn the pole in the same direction as the hands of a clock move. We call this a clockwise moment. If the weight was removed, the pole would move in the opposite direction to a clock's hands. We call this an anticlockwise moment. If the clockwise and anticlockwise moments are equal they are balanced.

Is the shaduf balanced?

Calculating forces

0.5 m

4 m

water bucket
50 N

weight
400 N

▲ **Beam for moment calculations**

Calculating moments							
	Weight (N)	Distance from pivot (m)	Moment (Nm)	Weight of water (N)	Distance from pivot (m)	Moment (Nm)	Balanced?
A	100	1	?	20	5	?	?
B	200	0.5	?	15	6	?	?
C	400	0.25	?	50	?	?	yes

Science at work

When architects design buildings they must make sure the moments balance or the buildings will fall down.

C Copy and complete the table, calculating the unknown moments. (Level 6)

Football stands

These photographs show old and new football stands. It is much easier to see the whole pitch from the new football stands without posts being in the way. This is achieved by using the principle of moments.

D Explain one way in which a football stadium roof could be designed so that it will not fall down if there are no posts to keep it up. (Level 7)

E Sam pushes with a force of 10 N, 2 m from the pivot of a seesaw. Amber pushes with a force of 20 N 1 m from the pivot on the same side of the pivot. Ryan is 3 m from the pivot on the other side. He pushes down with enough force to keep the seesaw level. (i) Draw a diagram to show the scenario. (ii) Calculate Ryan's force. (Level 8)

Keywords
lever, moment, pivot, principle of moments, turning effect

Learn about:

- why athletes analyse data
- using evidence to provide explanations

▶ The greatest distance wins gold

▼ The forces acting on a javelin

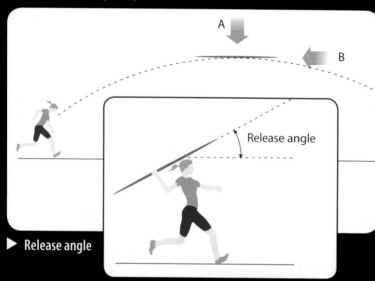

A

B

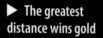
Release angle

▶ Release angle

Sue is a javelin thrower. She is training for the next Olympics. 'I think the track and field events are the most exciting,' she says. 'That's because there are no judges; the winners are the fastest runners or the longest throwers. In order to do my best, I analyse all aspects of my performance to try and identify areas for improvement.'

Throwing the javelin

To make the javelin travel as far as possible, Sue tries to give it as much speed as she can. Once she has let go, the javelin starts to slow down. There are two forces which limit how fast it will travel.

▼ Distance against release angle for a javelin

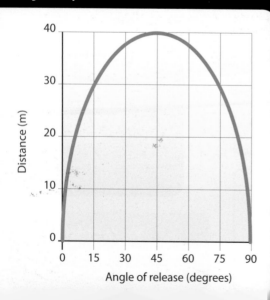

A (i) Name the forces A and B acting on the javelin.
(ii) How does the javelin make force B as small as possible? (Level 4)

As well as the speed of the javelin, the angle at which it is released has a big effect on how far it travels. This angle is called the **release angle** and the diagram shows what scientists mean by it. The graph shows how far Sue's javelin travels when she throws it with different release angles.

B (i) What is the maximum distance Sue throws a javelin?
(ii) At what angle should Sue release a javelin for maximum distance? (iii) Describe the relationship between distance and angle. (Level 5)

Focus on how science works

The long jump

Rachel is training for the long jump. In the long jump, Rachel is throwing herself rather than the javelin so she has a **take-off angle** rather than a release angle. The table shows the different distances she can jump with different take-off angles.

▲ Take-off angle affects distance travelled

Maximum distances at different take-off angles											
Take-off angle (degrees)	0	5	10	15	20	25	30	35	40	45	50	55
Distance (m)	0	4	6	7.5	8	8	7.2	5.8	4	3	2	1.5

C Plot the data from the table above on a graph. (i) Describe the relationship between distance and take-off angle. (ii) What is the best take-off angle to jump the longest distance? (Level 6)

Science at work

Javelins were originally used as weapons. A rhino shoulder blade fossil was found in a gravel quarry in England. Scientists dated it to 500,000 years ago and think it was wounded by a javelin.

D Why do you think that long jumpers do not jump the furthest at similar angles to those at which a javelin is thrown the furthest? (Level 7)

▶ Graph comparing the take-off speed to the take-off angle

Take-off angle and take-off speed

Scientists originally thought that the longest distance was achieved in the long jump if the take-off angle was 45 degrees. But you have seen from Rachel's take-off angle v distance table that it is not, but why?

Scientists measured the **take-off speeds** of long jumpers and the angle they jumped at. Their results are shown in the graph on the right.

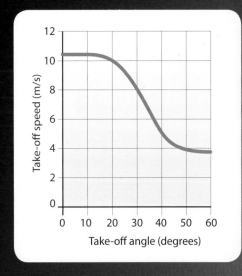

E Use the evidence (graph and data) to explain the angle of take-off most likely to result in a long distance. (Level 8)

Keywords
release angle, take-off angle, take-off speed

5.9 Guilty or not guilty?

Learn about:
- evaluating evidence to come to a decision
- justifying an opinion

Best Science Lesson Ever

Science at work

After someone is killed, a pathologist carries out a post-mortem to find out the exact cause of death.

▲ Who was responsible for the car crash?

Teenager killed in car crash,
Daily News, 6 February

Sarah Smith,16, was killed at 5pm today when the BMW she was a passenger in collided with a lorry in Church Lane. The BMW had been stolen earlier that day from a shopping centre. The driver, John Gunn, 18, admitted to the police that he stole the car, but denied that he caused the crash which killed sixth form student Sarah.

Before you start

You are going to play the part of a jury member in Courtroom 1. You are going to hear the police evidence and the witness statements and you are going to decide whether John Gunn was responsible for the crash or not.

What to do

You will need to organise yourselves into groups of four. In your groups, read the police report detailing the weather and vehicle conditions and the statements from the drivers and answer the questions.

Police accident report

Weather: wet; temperature: 1°C; sun low in the sky

The accident happened in a 13 m/s (30 mph) street

Car: brakes in good condition; tread on all tyres: 5–6 mm

Lorry: brakes in good condition; tread on front tyres: 5 mm, tread on back tyres: 1mm

(Note: min legal tread depth: 3 mm)

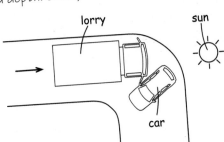

I was just having a laugh, driving around really fast and showing off. The lorry just hit me. I'm sorry Sarah's dead.

I started work at 6am and was on my last delivery. I was hoping to get back for the match. I was taking my time when the car came from nowhere. I braked hard but couldn't stop in time.'

The car came blasting along playing that awful boom boom music. It's no wonder he hit the lorry. Should be locked up I say!

A Which driver, John or the lorry driver, could have been distracted by the Sunlight? (Level 4)

B Would the lorry's tyre tread affect the thinking distance, braking distance or both? Explain your answer. (Level 5)

C From the lorry driver's statement, note down anything that might have affected his driving. From John's statement, note down anything that might have affected his driving. From the witness's statement, note down anything that might have affected John or the lorry driver. (Level 6)

D (i) Describe the speed–time graph of the BMW in as much detail as you can. (ii) Identify the discrepancy between the graph data and the statement of the witness. (Level 7)

E (i) Compare the lorry driver's statement with the speed–time graph from his computer and identify any discrepancies. (ii) What evidence is there on the graph that the lorry driver saw the car late? (iii) What evidence is there on the graph that the lorry's braking might have been affected by the poor tyres? (Level 8)

Discuss in your groups who you think was to blame.

In court, the police now present their evidence about how fast each vehicle was going as speed–time graphs. Take a look at them in your groups and answer the questions.

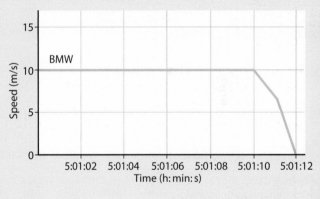

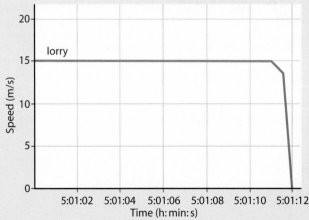

Discuss in your groups whether the speed data has changed your mind about who was to blame. Come to a final decision and feed back to the rest of the class giving reasons for your decision.

5.2

1. What two things do you need to measure to calculate an object's speed? (Level 4)
2. What does a constant slope on a distance–time graph tell you about an object's speed? (Level 5)
3. Look at this speed–time graph of Becca's shopping trip.

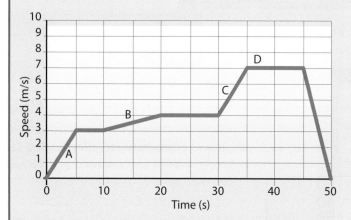

  a. During which part of the journey is Becca travelling the fastest? Explain your answer.

  b. What is happening during part D? (Level 6)

4. Imagine you are a radio commentator on the sprinter v dog race. Write a commentary of the race using a distance–time graph of the data in this table. (Level 7)

Sprinter v dog race

Time (s)	0	2	4	6	8	10
Distance (m) (sprinter)	0	20	40	60	80	100
Distance (m) (dog)	0	0	20	50	100	100

5. Sam takes part in a 20 km cycle race. The distance–time graph shows Sam's race.

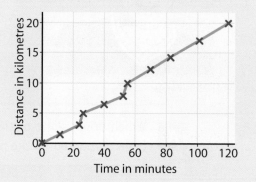

  a. How many sprints does Sam take part in? Explain your answer.

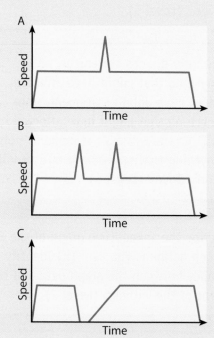

  b. Look at these three speed–time graphs. Which of the speed–time graphs shows Sam's race?

  c. Which of them shows a cyclist who took part in only one sprint?

  d. Which of them shows a cyclist who had a puncture? (Level 8)

5.3

1 Why do falling objects accelerate at first? (Level 4)
2 Describe how the speed changes during a parachute jump, from when the jumper first leaves the plane until when they land. (Level 5)
3 Look at the two jumpers in the diagram.

Why would jumper B fall faster through the air? (Level 6)
4 Emma asks ten of her friends if they have been injured using roller skates. One says she has broken her wrist and one has broken her arm falling over. She decides that this means that two in every ten people will break a bone roller-skating at some time. What is wrong with her conclusion? (Level 7)
5 An object falling through water has a far lower maximum speed than it has falling through the air. Explain why. (Level 8)

5.4

1 What is the relationship between the number of wheels a vehicle has and its pressure on the ground? (Level 4)
2 Why is it easier to push a pin into a drawing board than to push your finger into a drawing board? (Level 5)
3 Why do people let some of the air out of tyres when driving their car off-road on boggy ground? (Level 6)
4 You lay a piece of string with weights attached to the ends over a block of ice and leave it for a while. When you come back, the string has travelled through the ice. Explain why. (Level 7)
5 The ice truckers deliver 10 000 loads in a typical year. If two truckers die in a year then that would suggest a chance of being killed as 1 in 5000 deliveries. Explain how one driver could reduce his chances of being killed. (Level 8)

5.5

1 What will happen to the size of the force exerted by a hydraulic system if the output piston has a smaller area? (Level 4)
2 The rules for pressure in gases are the same as for pressure in liquids. What will the pressure be like at the top of a mountain compared to at sea level? (Level 5)
3 An input piston applies a pressure of $10\,N/cm^2$. If the pipe splits into two, what will the pressure be at each of the output pistons? (Level 6)
4 In a car's braking system, what do you think is the relationship between the distance an input piston moves compared to the distance an output piston moves? (Level 7)
5 An hydraulic system is used to open a valve on an oil pipeline. The pipeline travels deeper into the ocean as it goes further from land. Shaun says that the pressure in the hydraulic system will increase as the pipeline goes deeper. Is he right? Explain your answer. (Level 8)

5.6

1 When a balloon has a leak, the number of air particles in it decreases. What happens to the pressure? Explain your answer. (Level 4)

2 Look at Amber and Ryan's experiment on p 89. It has an anomalous result. What should they have done to try and reduce the chance of this happening, which would make their results more reliable? (Level 5)

3 If you push the plunger down on a syringe filled with air, what will happen to the volume and pressure of the air? (Level 6)

4 When you use a pump it gets hot. Use the particle model to explain why this happens. (Level 7)

5 If you blow up a beach ball, its volume will increase. What effect will this have on its pressure? (*Hint:* think about the particle model.) (Level 8)

5.7

1 What happens to the size of a moment if a load is moved away from the pivot? (Level 4)

2 A load is 5 m from the end of a crane.

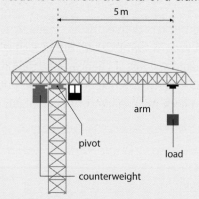

If it is moved towards the tower by 2.5 m, what will happen to its moment? (Level 5)

3 a Calculate the moments of the children on the seesaw.

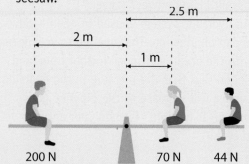

b Which way will the seesaw move? (Level 6)

4 Look at the diagram of a beam. What upward force must you provide to keep the beam level? (Level 7)

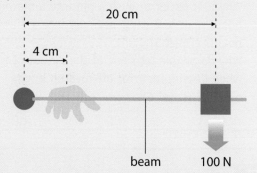

5

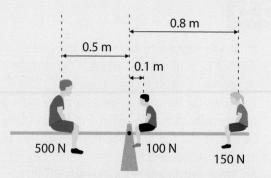

Is the seesaw balanced? If not, which side will go down? (*Hint:* treat each moment independently.) (Level 8)

5.8

1 What is the relationship between the force an athlete applies to a javelin and its speed through the air? (Level 4)

2 Look at the graph showing the distances the javelin is thrown at different release angles. What variables have not been considered when collecting this evidence? (Level 5)

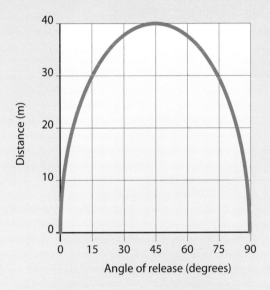

3 Look at the graph showing gold medal winning distances for the javelin at the Olympics.

Describe the graph in as much detail as possible. (Level 6)

4 Look at the graph on page 93 that shows take-off speeds and angles of long jumpers. Describe the relationship between take-off speeds and take-off angle. (Level 7)

5 Take a look at the graph of the javelin winning distances. Why do you think the Olympic governing body altered the design of the javelin after 1976? (Level 8)

5.9

1 Why might the temperature and weather increase the braking distance of the vehicles mentioned on pages 94–95? (Level 4)

2 Explain why it is important to look at the evidence in a crash before coming to a decision about who is to blame. (Level 5)

3 Comment on the reliability of the witness to the crash. Why could her evidence be less reliable than the police statement? (Level 6)

4 If the accident had happened before the first delivery of the day, the lorry would have decelerated less than it did at 5pm. Explain why. (Level 7)

5 The police have been called to a crash. A motorcyclist swerved to avoid hitting a dog. He hit a lamppost and was killed. Explain what pieces of evidence the police need to obtain and why. (Level 8)

6.1 A mystery in Space

It's hard to imagine but there are objects in Space that are brighter than a trillion stars.

Astronomers first began spotting these incredibly bright objects in the 1960s. They could see they were powerful and very far away – but what were they? No one could imagine how an object could give out so much light energy. These objects were so bright that scientists decided they couldn't work in the same way as stars like the Sun. Astronomers named the objects quasars – but naming them didn't solve the mystery of what they were.

Forty years later, astronomers still can't agree on how quasars work. But they have developed a model to explain how they could produce this massive amount of energy. In their model a quasar forms when a monster black hole in the middle of a galaxy sucks in lots of stardust. As the dust spirals into the black hole, a huge amount of energy is released.

If they are right it means the black hole at the centre of a big quasar is devouring the equivalent mass of a thousand stars per year.

Now try these

- The Moon orbits the Earth but what force holds it in its orbit?

- Quasars can be millions of light years away. Why can astronomers see the light that travels to us from them?

- The time a planet takes to orbit the Sun changes as you move away from the Sun. Does it get slower or faster?

Coming up in this Chapter ...

Artificial satellites play an important role in everyday life.

The sun exerts a force of gravitational attraction on the Earth.

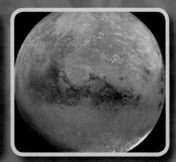

Mars is the planet nearest to Earth. What keeps the planets in orbit around the Sun?

Humans have only travelled as far as the Moon, but we've sent probes to other planets.

Learn about:

- mass, distance and the force of gravitational attraction
- how scientists' ideas are used by others to work out problems

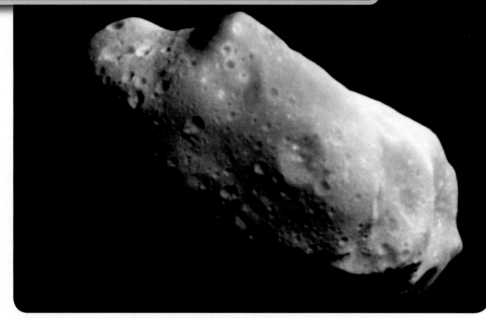

▲ Rocky asteroid in space

Amazing fact

In 2000 humans landed a spacecraft on an asteroid, called Eros, for the first time. Eros is 33 km in length and it sometimes passes close to Earth during its orbit around the sun of 643 Earth-days.

Asteroids are lumps of rock in Space too small to be a moon or planet. If you have two asteroids in Space and leave them floating close to each other without any other forces acting on them they will slowly move together. This is because of the gravitational forces acting between them.

What is gravitational attraction?

Every object with mass exerts a force of gravitational attraction on every other object with mass. The more the mass the greater the force.

| A | Compare the forces of gravitational attraction on you from your desk and from the Earth. (*Hint:* think about the mass of each object.) (Level 4) |

Right now, your desk is pulling you and you are pulling your desk. Why don't you move towards it?

| B | People sometimes say there is no gravity in Space between the Earth and the Moon. Why is this wrong? (Level 5) |

Moving around

The force of gravitational attraction between the Earth and the Moon pulls the Moon towards the Earth. But at the same time the Moon is moving fast through Space. The result of the pulling force is to change the Moon's path so that it **orbits** around and around the Earth.

In the same way the planets in the Solar System are being pulled towards the Sun but are also travelling fast through Space. The result is that they orbit the Sun.

C Explain why the Earth orbits the Sun. (Level 6)

A massive idea

Isaac Newton said that the gravitational attraction between two objects depends on:

- how big a mass they each have – a larger mass means a bigger force of gravitational attraction
- how close they are – it is stronger when two objects are closer and weaker when they are further apart.

D Describe and explain the strength of the forces of gravitational attraction acting on the Earth from: (i) Neptune (ii) the Sun. (Level 7)

▲ Planets such as Venus (above) are pulled towards the Sun but also travel fast through Space

Making calculations

You can calculate the force of gravitational attraction between two objects using Newton's equation. You need to know the masses of the two objects plus their distance apart. You also need a number called **G**.

$$\text{force} = \frac{\text{mass of first object} \times \text{mass of second object} \times G}{\text{distance apart} \times \text{distance apart}}$$

Finding G

In 1798 Henry Cavendish wanted to find out the value of G. G is a number that never changes and is needed in most gravity calculations. So Cavendish got two huge masses and measured the force of gravitational attraction between them. He knew their distance apart and the sizes of the masses and calculated G. It's different to g (lower case) which refers to the acceleration due to gravity on Earth.

The mass of the Earth

Cavendish then used Newton's equation to find out the mass of the Earth for the first time. To do this he needed the radius of the Earth. Luckily for him this had been worked out by a scientist called Erastosthenes in ancient Egypt. Cavendish calculated that the Earth's mass is 6 000 000 000 000 000 000 000 000 kg. This figure has been confirmed since and is used by scientists studying planetary motions and forces.

▲ To discover G, Cavendish used a huge dumbbell hanging from his ceiling

E The Earth's radius is 6356 km. The volume of a sphere is $4/3 \times \pi \times r^3$ where π is about 3.14 and r is the radius. Calculate the Earth's volume. (Level 8)

Keywords
asteroid, G, orbit

Learn about:

- how artificial satellites get into and stay in orbit
- the ways that satellite technology can help you

▲ An artist's impression of an asteroid striking the Earth. Using a satellite, scientists found a huge asteroid crater beneath Antarctica's icy surface

What's the connection between an enormous crater under the Antarctic ice and 74 long-lost medieval temples in Cambodia? They were both found with the help of **artificial satellites**.

Types of satellites and their uses

Artificial satellites are used in many ways. The UK is a world-leader when it comes to designing and manufacturing satellites. It's a high-tech, money-making business that grows larger every year.

- **Communications satellites** send radio, TV and telephone signals around the World.
- Some **exploration satellites** orbit the Earth and search Space (like the Hubble telescope), while others orbit the other planets in our Solar System.
- **Navigation satellites** help cars, ships and planes find their position by sending information to GPS navigation systems.
- **Observation satellites** are used for spying and to observe nature. Weather forecasting relies on a large number of observation satellites to get measurements and pictures.

> **A** Jack parks his car, uses his mobile phone to call his friend and says according to the GPS, he's 10 minutes away. Which types of satellite have just helped him? (Level 4)

Sputnik

The first artificial satellite to go into Space was called Sputnik. It was launched on a missile by the Russians in 1957. Sputnik had no rockets, so how could it stay up in Space?

Isaac Newton realised that if you shoot a cannon ball from a cannon on a hilltop it will curve down and hit the Earth. But if the cannon ball moves fast enough the Earth curves away from the cannon ball before the ball lands, allowing it to orbit the Earth.

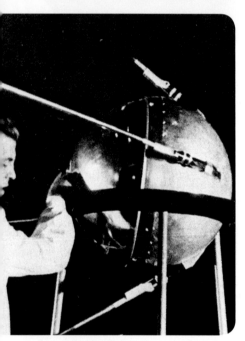

▲ Sputnik was the size of a beach ball

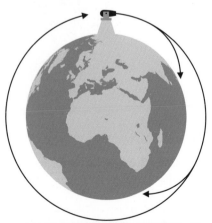

▲ Newton thought about the paths of cannon balls shot from a cannon and realised they could go into orbit if they moved fast enough

B (i) What kind of force is created by air rubbing against a moving satellite? (ii) The Earth produces a force that pulls on the satellite. What is the force and in which direction is this force pulling? (Level 5)

Launching satellites

Sputnik was carried into Space by a rocket and was then released. It was travelling at a speed of about 29 000 km/h as it went into orbit. After 3 months in orbit, its speed dropped and it re-entered Earth's atmosphere. It then burnt up as it fell back to the ground.

Today satellites are carried into Space by rockets. The rockets use their large thrusters to travel straight up. The thrusters eject gas downwards and this pushes the rocket upwards. It works in the same way that a balloon flies around the room if you release it and the neck is not tied. The force of the thrusters has to be larger than the force of gravitational attraction pulling the rocket back to Earth.

As the rocket climbs, small thrusters fire and rotate the craft so that the engines push the rocket into an orbit around the Earth instead of moving straight away from it. The satellite is then released. It will stay in orbit as long as it is going fast enough.

Science at work

Lots of British aerospace engineers work on international projects to build, maintain and repair satellites and Space vehicles.

◀ Artificial satellites are carried into Space by rockets

C As a rocket travels upwards, it expels gas. How does this change the mass of the rocket and the amount of gravitational force acting on it? (Level 6)

D As the rocket travels upwards, it moves away from the centre of the Earth. How does this affect the gravitational force on the rocket? (Level 7)

E Rockets burn fuel very fast on lift-off. As they climb the rocket's acceleration increases even though the thrust doesn't get any bigger. Explain why this is by referring to the changing mass of the rocket and the forces on it. (Level 8)

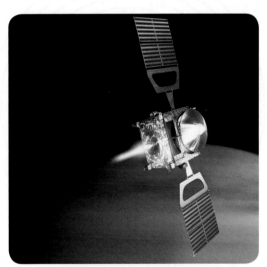

▲ British aerospace engineers build instruments for satellites like the Venus Express

Keywords
artificial satellite,
communications satellite,
exploration satellite,
navigation satellite,
observation satellite

6.4 What can you see?

Learn about:

- different models of the Solar System and how beliefs influenced them
- how evidence from observations helps improve models
- how scientists get evidence about the Universe now

▲ Can zebras make you question your preconceptions?

You stand on the street and a zebra runs past, followed by a man wearing a jacket that says 'London Zoo'. What do you think is going on? As you look at the world around, you use your existing knowledge and beliefs to help you make sense of what you see. In this case, you probably drew on your knowledge of zoos to say that the zebra had escaped from one.

Explaining the Universe

For thousands of years people have used their observations and beliefs to explain the movements they see in the night sky. In 550 BC Pythagoras believed that everything was made of four materials, with fire being the most important. His model had a fire at the centre of the Universe with everything, including the Sun, moving around it.

One hundred years later Plato observed that from Earth we see the Sun and planets apparently moving around us. He came up with a **geocentric** model, with the Earth at the centre of the Universe. Aristotle was Plato's pupil. In his model stars and planets were attached to 56 'celestial spheres' which surround the Earth.

▲ Aristotle's model of the Universe had the Earth at the centre

A Scientists now know that forces of gravitational attraction hold the planets in their orbits. In Aristotle's model, what kept the planets in place? (Level 4)

Making observations

In about 100 AD, Ptolemy observed that some planets seem to do a slow loop-the-loop as they move across the sky. He used Aristotle's model and added a small sphere to each celestial sphere so that each planet performed a loop during its circuit.

B Why did Ptolemy say his model was better than Aristotle's model? (Level 5)

Ptolemy's model was accepted for thousands of years. It explained people's observations of the sky and fitted with their religious belief that the Earth was at the centre of the Universe.

In the sixteenth century, Copernicus spent 30 years observing the night sky. He devised a **heliocentric** model of the Solar System which had the Sun at the centre. In 1609 Galileo invented the telescope. Now astronomers could test their models against observations.

A few decades later Kepler used observations to make the heliocentric model better by working out that planets move in **elliptical orbits** around the Sun. An ellipse is like a squashed circle.

C Do you think that the belief that heaven is located around the Earth is a belief that began during the time of the heliocentric or geocentric model? (Level 6)

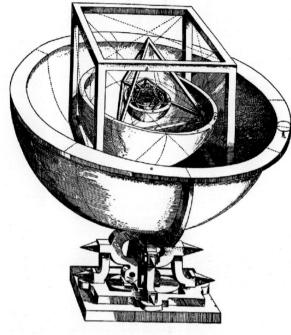

▲ Kepler's model of the Solar System had the Sun at the centre and the planets moving in elliptical obits around it

Astronomy today

Using telescopes and Space exploration, astronomers have gathered more evidence to support Kepler's heliocentric model. This model guides astronomers when they use powerful telescopes to study stars beyond our Sun. They have found that many other stars have planets.

In observing the Universe, scientists have discovered other **galaxies**. So they have had to construct new, more complicated models to explain these observations. Meanwhile, engineers and scientists continue to work on new projects to take people into Space. These include a project to set up a permanent base on the Moon and a project to take people to Mars for the first time.

◄ Radio telescopes collect data during the day and night and produce highly detailed views of the Universe

D The idea of galaxies as clusters of billions of stars doesn't feature in early models of the Universe. Use this as an example to show the link between observations and models. (Level 7)

E If a star has a massive planet nearby, the planet can be detected by a wobble in the star's light as the planet moves around and pulls the star. Why is it harder to detect a small planet orbiting the same star? (Level 8)

Keywords
elliptical orbit, galaxy, geocentric, heliocentric

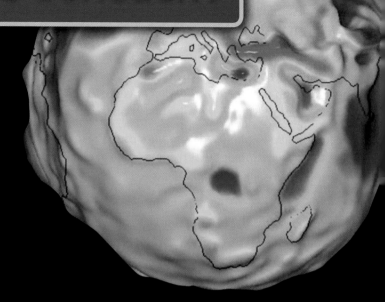

Learn about:

- how gravity is different depending on where you stand
- why scientists measure gravitational forces around the Earth

...m is standing ...a sandstone ...ck. This is light ...d so doesn't ...ll Sam strongly

His friend Mike is standing on an iron rock. This is dense and pulls Mike down strongly

The rocks further from the boys' feet are also pulling them, but they are more distant, they produce less force

▲ The force of gravitational attraction is greater when you stand on a dense material

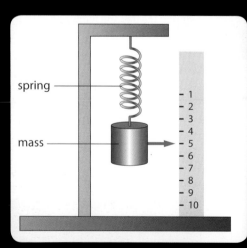

spring

mass

▲ The most common type of gravimeter has a mass hanging on a spring

This is a **gravity map** of the Earth. You may think that the force of gravitational attraction is the same all over the Earth, but it's not.

At the Earth's surface, the Earth pulls objects downwards with a force of 9.8 Newtons on every kg of mass. But this is an average. The exact force changes from place to place, depending on where you are standing and what you are standing on.

Gravity surveys

Rocks are made from different materials. Some are made of sand while others contain denser materials like iron. A dense material is one that is very heavy for its size. Think of a block of iron compared with a block of polystyrene. When you stand on rock that has lots of iron in it you are pulled down more strongly than if you stand on a rock made mostly of sand.

A A block of iron and a block of polystyrene are the same size. (i) Which block has more mass? (ii) Which provides the greater force of gravitational attraction? (Level 4)

Geologists carry out **gravity surveys** to investigate these little differences in gravitational attraction. They use a spring with a mass on the end to measure the force of gravitational attraction in each place. This is called a **gravimeter**. The stronger the force, the more the spring stretches as the mass is pulled down.

B The force on a 1 kg block at the Earth's surface is on average 9.8 Newtons. (i) What is the force on a 50 kg pupil? (ii) What are the weights of the block and the pupil? (Level 5)

Hidden secrets

Gravity surveys are useful because they help scientists to work out what is below the surface without having to dig or drill. Gravity surveys have revealed underground springs, rivers and volcanic basins. They have also provided evidence that the Antarctic ice sheet is losing ice.

- **Geophysicists** use gravity surveys to look for underground rock movements that might show that an earthquake is on its way.
- **Oceanographers** do regular gravity surveys to spot changes in ocean currents and changes in climate.
- **Archaeologists** sometimes use gravity surveys to look at the remains of walls and buildings underground and decide where to investigate.

▲ What lies below the ice? A gravity survey can provide answers

The view from Space

Satellites can now measure gravity variations from Space to produce gravity maps like the one of the Earth. The red parts are areas of higher gravity.

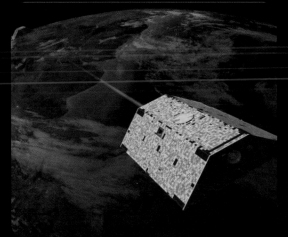

Interesting fact

A gravimeter was recently fitted to an Australian F-27 aircraft and used to gather data about the Great Barrier Reef.

◀ The GRACE satellites carry out gravity surveys of the Earth

C (i) Suggest why scientists use colours rather than numbers on the map to represent the changes in gravity. (ii) What is an advantage of presenting the data numerically? (Level 6)

The photo shows a gravity map of a meteorite crater in Antarctica. Scientists used a model to work out what happened. In their model a meteorite slammed into the Earth, making a gigantic crater and throwing dense rock from deeper in the Earth into the air. The dense rock fell into the crater and later the whole area was covered in ice.

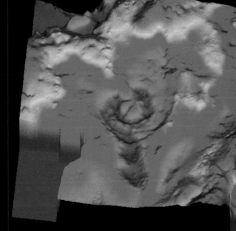

▲ Gravity map of crater in the Antarctic

D Create a key to go with the gravity map of Antarctica. Suggest which colours represent medium, low and very low gravity areas. (Level 7)

E As well as showing areas of high density, gravity maps also show the locations of mountains and valleys. Why would a mountain appear different to a valley? (Level 8)

Keywords
archaeologist, geophysicist, gravimeter, gravity map, gravity survey, oceanographer

Assess your progress

6.2

1 What pieces of information and/or ideas by other scientists did Cavendish need in order to work out the mass of the Earth? (Level 4)

2 If you hold an apple over the ground and let go, it falls to Earth and doesn't fall towards you. Why? (Level 5)

3 The Sun's force of gravitational attraction causes a tidal effect but it is not as noticeable as the tidal effect due to the Moon's gravitational attraction. Suggest why this is. (Level 6)

4 Why did Cavendish choose to place huge masses on the dumbbell in his experiment? (Level 7)

5 Your weight on Jupiter would be about double your weight on Earth. Jupiter has a huge radius and is made mostly of gas. Earth has a smaller radius but is made mostly of rock. The further you are from a planet's centre, the lower the gravitational force. Explain why your weight would not be as much on Jupiter as it would be on a rocky planet with the same mass as Jupiter. (Level 8)

6.3

1 Look at the graph of orbital speed against distance from the Sun.

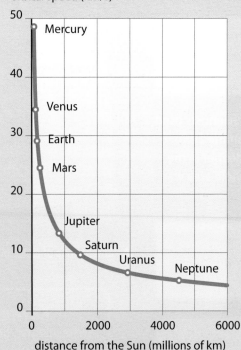

a Where is the Sun on the graph? (Level 4)
b Which planet moves about three times faster than Saturn? (Level 5)

2 The Moon is a natural satellite of the Earth. In what way is the Moon similar to an artificial satellite of the Earth (Level 6)

3 Suppose a satellite is in an orbit where air is present but thin. Explain why the satellite must frequently fire booster rockets and what will happen if it does not. (Level 7)

4 Compare the gravitational forces of attraction that are at work on a satellite in a low-altitude orbit with one in a high-altitude orbit. (The altitude of a satellite refers to its distance from the Earth's surface.) (Level 8)

6.4

1 Look at pages 106–107. Two main types of model of the Solar System are described. What terms are used to describe them and what do the terms mean? (Level 4)

2 Explain why the Earth's rotation led astronomers to create a geocentric model of the Solar System. (Level 5)

3 'If you get a job as an astronomer, you end up working nights'. Discuss this comment by describing the typical work of a modern astronomer. (Level 6)

4 Galileo became unpopular with religious leaders for arguing that Copernicus's model of the Solar System was correct. Why? (Level 7)

5 In Aristotle's model, the spheres increase gradually in size, with the Sun's sphere just a few steps beyond the Moon's sphere. Explain how Aristotle's observations of the Sun and Moon and of a solar eclipse might lead him to draw this conclusion. (Level 8)

6.5

1 List some features that can be identified using a gravity survey. (Level 4)

2 When scientists studied the gravity map of Antarctica they found a circular area of higher density. Why did this suggest that there may have been a meteorite impact in that area? (Level 5)

3 A climber with a 10 kg rucksack reaches the top of Everest. Would the force of gravitational attraction acting on the rucksack be more or less at the top of the mountain than it was at the bottom? Explain your answer. (Level 6)

4 A scientist is searching for a box filled with gold.
 a How could an aerial gravity survey help her find the box?
 b What will the box look like on the gravity map? (Level 7)

5 A gravity map of a school playing field reveals a large rectangle with low gravity. The head teacher thinks there was once a swimming pool in the grounds. He is worried that it was not properly filled in. What is the evidence for his theory? (Level 8)

Niagara Falls is one of most powerful waterfalls in the world. Many daredevils have seen the falls as a challenge. In 1901 Annie Taylor was the first person to go over the falls in a barrel and survive. In 1920 Englishman Charles G. Stephens was not so lucky. When his barrel was recovered, only his right arm was found inside.

A person in a barrel at the top of the Niagara Falls has about 45 000 joules of gravitational potential energy due to being high up. The water at the top of the falls also has potential energy. Energy is never created or destroyed. It is transferred from one form to another. As the water falls the potential energy is transferred as kinetic energy. Some of the kinetic energy is transferred as sound energy when the falling water hits the river below, creating a roar. Some of the kinetic energy is transferred as heat energy and makes the water temperature rise. This effect was predicted and tested by the scientist James Joule.

Now try these

- What energy transfers take place in a battery-powered fan?

- Where does the energy come from to move a barrel over the Niagara Falls?

- How many different ways can you think of for generating electricity?

Coming up in this Chapter ...

James Joule measured the temperature of waterfalls to show that it increased as the water fell

A bonfire transfers stored chemical energy into heat and light energy

Scientists think that waddling is the most energy-efficient way for penguins to move

You can save energy by switching off lights when you don't need them

Animals, models and energy

Learn about:

- energy conservation and dissipation
- how scientists investigate energy efficiency

▲ Knowing the most efficient way to walk helps scientists to design better robots

Why do some birds fly in a V formation? Why does your leg swing like a pendulum when you walk? The answer to both questions is: to be energy efficient. The **energy efficiency** of an organism or a machine is the percentage of energy going in that is transferred as useful forms.

Efficient feet

When you walk you swing each leg forward with a straight knee like a pendulum. Scientists wanted to find out why so they created a virtual person on a computer and tested out different ways to walk. The computer model showed that the so-called pendulum swing is the walk that is the most energy efficient.

Pelican puzzle

Another team of scientists predicted that some birds fly in a V formation to be energy efficient, but didn't know how to prove it. Bird flight is too complicated to model on a computer so they found a wildlife film crew who were training some pelicans to fly over a boat.

The scientists fixed tiny heart monitors to the birds to tell the scientists how hard the birds' muscles were working as they flew. They were then able to record and compare the energy the birds used to fly in different patterns and so showed that their prediction was correct.

> **A** Scientists used different methods to investigate the energy efficiency of humans and pelicans – what were they? (Level 4)

Energy transfers

The unit of energy is the **joule (J)**. One joule is not much energy and most transfers are described in **kilojoules (kJ)**. To walk a kilometre, you transfer about 150 000 J or 150 kJ of stored energy as heat energy and kinetic energy.

> **B** Jane is listening to her iPod and drops it. What energy transfers take place? (Level 5)

> **C** You transfer about the same amount of energy to walk a kilometre as to run a kilometre. If you run three times faster than you walk, how much faster are you transferring energy when you run? (Level 6)

Energy efficiency

Scientists use the idea that all energy in the Universe is **conserved**, which means it can never be destroyed or created. This idea can help you to work out the energy efficiency of a machine.

A traditional light bulb requires 100 joules of electrical energy every second and gives out 5 joules of light. The remaining electrical energy is transferred as unwanted heat. If you work out the percentage of the electrical energy that is transferred as light, this tells you the energy efficiency of the bulb.

> **D** (i) What percentage of the electrical energy is transferred as unwanted heat by the light bulb?
> (ii) What is the energy efficiency of the light bulb? (Level 7)

In comparison a compact fluorescent bulb requires 10–20 joules of electrical energy per second but still gives out 5 joules of light. It is more energy efficient which saves money.

Energy dissipation

Scientists say that the traditional light bulb **dissipates** energy as unwanted heat. You can measure how much electrical energy goes into a light bulb and how much light energy comes out. The difference between these two amounts tells you how much energy is dissipated.

By identifying where and why the dissipated energy is transferred scientists and engineers can change their designs to make machines and gadgets as efficient as possible.

> **E** A website says that loft insulation pays for itself in about 2 years. Think about electricity powered heating and refer to electrical energy and any relevant energy transfers to explain the basis of this claim. (Level 8)

▲ An iPod transfers stored chemical energy as electrical energy and then transfers this as sound and heat

▲ Night diving is one of the greatest excitements for a diver and requires a bright, long-lasting torch

Interesting fact

A bicycle is a very energy efficient form of transportation. A cyclist requires 20 to 100 times less energy than a car to cover the same distance.

Keywords

energy conservation, energy dissipation, energy efficiency, joule (J), kilojoule (kJ)

7.3 Electricity and energy

Learn about:

- how voltage and energy are related
- energy transfers in electrical circuits
- a model to describe voltage and energy

▲ Electric shocks can injure or kill people

Each year more than 100 people in Britain are killed by electric shocks and more than 2000 are killed or injured in electrical fires. An electricity supply with a high **voltage** is more dangerous than one with a low voltage. Voltage is measured in volts (V).

What is voltage?

Voltage is a measure of the difference in electrical energy between two points in a circuit. It is also called **potential difference**. Use a voltmeter in a circuit to show that the voltage goes up across the cells. The **current** has more energy as it leaves the cells. At each component, electrical energy is transferred from the current. There is a voltage drop across each component, which you can also measure using the voltmeter.

A What happens to the flow of electrical energy around a circuit when you use a switch to open the circuit? (Level 4)

A model of voltage

Imagine a mountain. A barrow of pebbles is pushed to the top. Then the barrow is tipped up so that the pebbles roll down in an avalanche. As the pebbles roll down the mountain, they speed up. The more pebbles and the faster they go, the more harm they will cause if they hit you at the bottom.

In this model, the moving pebbles represent current. The height of the mountain represents the voltage of the supply. The energy required to lift the pebbles up the mountain comes from the supply.

▲ The faster the pebbles go, the more harm they will cause at the bottom. This model shows that a higher voltage supply can produce a more energetic and so painful electric shock

B Why do the pebbles in the model have more energy if they fall from the top of a tall mountain rather than from the top of a smaller mountain? (Level 5)

Modelling an electrical circuit

You can use the same model of a mountain to model how a circuit works. This time, the pebbles roll down from the top of the mountain along ramps. Each ramp represents a component in the circuit.

Circuit	Model
1 The cell transfers energy to the current.	1 A crane lifts the pebbles to the top of the mountain.
2 The current travels along a wire.	2 The pebbles roll down a slope.
3 The current passes through the bulb. The bulb has **resistance** so energy is transferred.	3 The pebbles get to a ramp. You'd expect them to speed up as they roll down but this ramp has paddle wheels mounted in the walls. Energy is transferred from the pebbles to the paddle wheels. The length of the downward ramp represents the resistance of the bulb.
4 The current passes through the buzzer. The buzzer has more resistance than the bulb so more energy is transferred.	4 The pebbles get to another ramp. The ramp has paddle wheels. This ramp is longer. Rolling down a long ramp transfers more energy than rolling down a short one.

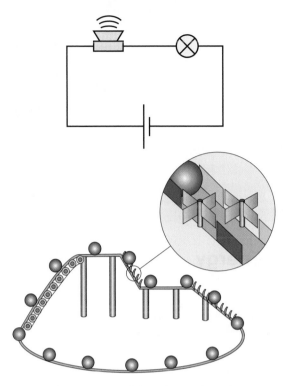

▲ You can model an electrical circuit using height to represent voltage

C A circuit has one cell. Explain why adding another cell increases the energy transferred to the current. (Level 6)

D Use the pebble and mountain model to explain why a very small current does not transfer much energy to the components in an electrical circuit. (Level 7)

Once they've travelled down all the ramps, the pebbles are at ground level. They are ready to be lifted by the crane and begin again.

Adding voltage

If you add the voltages of the components in a series circuit they equal the voltage of the supply.

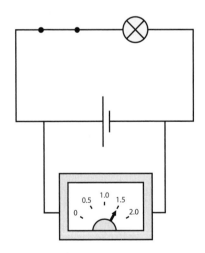

▲ The voltage across the cell is 1.5 V, a voltage gain. The voltage drops by 1.5 V across the bulb

E A series circuit has two identical bulbs and one buzzer which has twice the resistance of one of the bulbs. It has an 8 V cell. What is the voltage of each component? (Level 8)

Keywords
current, potential difference, resistance, voltage

Learn about:

- Sankey diagrams
- how scientific information guides people's buying choices
- what power is

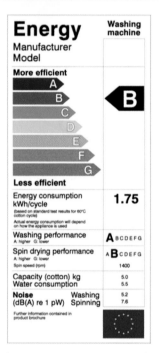

▲ A European Energy Label for a washing machine

▲ This washing machine is powered by pedalling but most washing machines use electricity

Your family is going to buy a new washing machine. You are charged for every unit of electrical energy you take from the mains supply so a more efficient machine uses less electricity and costs less to run.

Energy labels

All home appliances, including washing machines, now have a **European Energy Label** which shows the efficiency of the machine. The **efficiency rating** is at the top of the label. A machine with an A rating is more efficient and dissipates less energy than one with a B rating and so on down the scale.

When these labels were first introduced people were shocked to see that different machines required very different amounts of energy to run. Less efficient washing machines dissipated more energy by transferring it as useless noise and vibrations. The flow diagram shows the energy transfers for a washing machine.

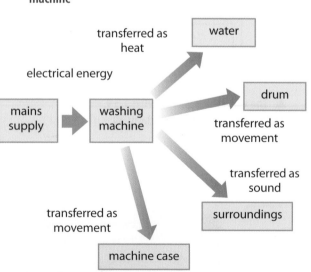

▲ Energy transfers that take place in a washing machine

> **A** Use the flow diagram to explain why cutting down on energy dissipated as vibration and noise can reduce the amount of electrical energy used. (*Hint*: Assume that the energy to move the drum and heat the water is fixed.) (Level 4)

Once manufacturers saw that buyers were checking the European Energy Labels they reduced the transfer of energy as noise and vibration and then looked for more ways to reduce the energy dissipated.

> **B** A manufacturer reduces the amount of water a machine uses. This reduces the amount of energy needed to heat the water. Looking at the flow diagram, will this reduce the amount of electrical energy used? (Level 5)

Sankey diagrams

Sankey diagrams show the energy transfers that take place in a machine. The width of each block or arrow represents the amount of energy in that form. Energy is always conserved so the total width of all the lines added together stays the same. The Sankey diagram below shows the energy transfers that take place in a washing machine.

C How does a Sankey diagram convey the idea that energy is never 'lost'? (Level 6)

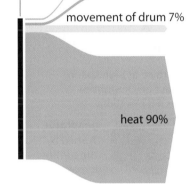

◀ Sankey diagram of a washing machine

D The energy entering the washing machine is electrical. (i) How much energy is dissipated as unwanted sound and movement? (ii) What form of energy enters a pedal-powered machine? (Level 7)

▶ No machine is 100% efficient. This Sankey diagram of a TV shows that 50% of the energy is dissipated as heat

Power

Energy is the ability to do work. The **power** of something tells you how quickly that work is done. The unit of power is the **watt (W)**. One watt is one joule per second. One **kilowatt (kW)** is 1000 joules per second. A traditional light bulb takes 60 joules per second of electrical energy and transfers it as light and heat. So it takes power at 60 W.

The power and energy needs of some appliances

Appliance	Power (watts)	Time switched on	Total energy (joules)
electric kettle	1000	5 minutes	300 000
hair dryer	1400	5 minutes	420 000
TV	300	2 hours	2 160 000
washing machine	1000–2000	1 hour	3 600 000– 7 200 000
compact fluorescent bulb	15	4 hours	216 000
traditional bulb	60	4 hours	864 000

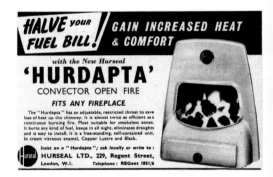
▲ Saving money by saving energy has always been popular, as this advert from 1955 shows

E Jo has a hairdryer with two settings, hot and cool. The cool setting draws 400 W of power and the hot draws 1400 W. If it takes 5 minutes to dry her hair on hot, what is the maximum time it should take on cool to be more energy-efficient? (Level 8)

Keywords
efficiency rating, European Energy Label, kilowatt (kW), power, Sankey diagram, watt (W)

Learn about:
- how power stations work
- the energy efficiency of different power stations

▲ We rely on having electricity available to run modern gadgets

One hundred years ago not many houses in the UK had electricity. Think about how many times a day you use electricity. Without reliable energy supplies your life would be much harder.

Providing electricity

A lot of electricity is produced at large **power stations** including **fossil-fuel power stations**, **hydroelectric power stations** and **nuclear power stations**. They may all seem different but they can be simplified into three main stages. Each power station needs a source of energy. Fossil-fuel power stations use chemical energy stored in fossil fuels such as coal, oil and gas.

> **A** What types of power stations do not use chemical energy? (Level 4)

Inside a power station

The photo shows inside the turbine hall of a fossil-fuel power station. First the fuel is burnt to transfer energy as heat. This heat is transferred to the water in the **boiler**, turning it into steam. The steam turns the turbine blades.

The **turbine** is connected to a **generator**. When the generator turns it produces electricity.

Each stage of a power station transfers energy to the next stage. Along the way some energy is dissipated as sound and heat. Eventually the remaining energy is transferred as electrical energy.

You can model how they work using a kettle, a child's spinning toy and a bicycle dynamo.

boiler
Thermal energy turns water into steam

turbine
The steam turns the turbine at high speed. It has to be pure because any impurities could break the blades if it hits them

generator
Turned by the turbine, it makes electricity

fuel
Chemical energy to thermal as fuel is burnt

cooling towers
The steam is condensed back into water in the cooling towers, then returned to the boiler

▲ How a power station works

▲ Inside the turbine hall of a power station

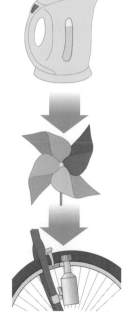

▲ Modelling a power station

> **B** What forms of energy are dissipated in a fossil-fuel power station? (Level 5)

How efficient?

An efficient fossil-fuel power station transfers as much of the chemical energy in the fuel as electrical energy as possible. Making power stations more efficient can help make electricity cheaper to generate and use. Look at the Sankey diagrams which show the energy transfers through a wind turbine, solar cell and a nuclear power station.

> **C** Cooling towers decrease the temperature of the hot water in fossil-fuel power stations. What else could the hot water be used for? (Level 6)

> **D** A hydroelectric power station uses moving water to turn the turbine. Why do you think this is much more efficient than a fossil-fuel power station? (Level 7)

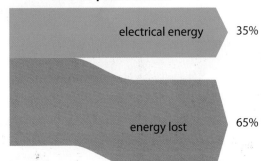

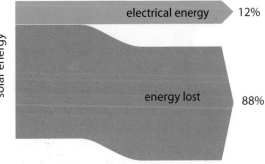

wind turbines

electrical energy — 35%

energy lost as sound, friction, heat — 65%

wind energy

solar cell

electrical energy — 12%

energy lost — 88%

solar energy

▶ **A comparison of different types of electrical energy generators**

nuclear power station

electrical energy — 35%

energy lost — 65%

nuclear fuel

Free electricity?

Sunlight can be used to generate electricity in different ways. **Solar panels** can transfer the energy in sunlight directly as electrical energy. Mirrors can also be used to reflect solar power and heat water. This water is then used to spin turbines in the same way as any other power station.

Wind farms use turbines to spin generators without the need for heating water. This means less energy is dissipated as heat.

Go nuclear

Nuclear power stations use the heat given off by **radioactive** uranium to heat water and turn it to steam. This then turns turbines in the usual way to generate electricity.

> **E** Nuclear fuel costs money to produce and then dispose of safely. Wind and water are free and renewable sources of energy. All types of power stations cost money to build and maintain. Using this information and the Sankey diagrams, which power station would you choose to produce your electricity? Explain why. (Level 8)

Science at work

Michael Faraday spent 10 years trying to come up with a device that turned movement into electricity. He succeeded in 1832.

Keywords

boiler, fossil-fuel power station, generator, hydroelectric power station, power station, nuclear power station, radioactive, solar panel, turbine, wind farm

7.6 Blowing in the wind?

Learn about:
- what people think about wind farms
- analysing evidence about the efficiency of wind farms

▲ Are wind farms the answer to our energy needs?

Fossil fuels are running out and cause pollution. Nuclear energy doesn't pollute but the waste it produces is hard to dispose of. Some scientists think that wind farms are the answer to our future energy needs, but others think that they are inefficient and have too many problems.

Opinions for and against wind farms

Wind farms do not cause acid rain.

They don't produce greenhouse gases.

They use a renewable energy source.

We won't have to worry about other countries not selling us oil and gas.

A (i) Rank the opinions of the people who are for wind farms in order of importance.
(ii) Write a sentence or two explaining your first and second choice. (Level 4)

Wind farms can be put on hilltops that are difficult to grow crops on.

Wind farms take up a lot of land compared to other power stations.

Wind farms spoil the countryside.

They only work when it is windy. What happens on days with no wind?

Birds can fly into them and get killed.

They don't produce very much electricity compared to other types of power stations.

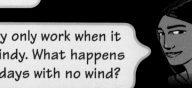

Considering the evidence

Wind turbines do not produce very much electricity, so you need a lot of them to replace a fossil fuel or nuclear power station.

A typical power station produces 520 megawatts (MW) of energy. A megawatt is 1000 kilowatts. It also takes up an area of about 1 km². This is about the size of a village. A typical wind turbine produces 2 megawatts (MW) of energy. When wind turbines are put together they have to be spaced out so they don't block the wind from each other. Each turbine needs an area of 320 000 m².

B How many wind turbines can be placed in the same space as a typical power station? (1 km = 1000 m) (Level 5)

C (i) How many wind turbines would it take to replace a typical power station? (ii) How much land would these wind turbines need? (Level 6)

D A turbine that is rated at 2 MW only produces this in the right conditions. What factors affect how much energy a turbine generates? (Level 7)

Wind speed

Wind turbines only transfer kinetic energy from the wind if it is blowing at the correct speed. Look at the graph showing average energy output of a typical turbine. The table shows the average wind speed in different parts of the UK.

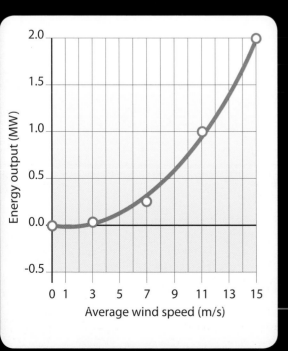

▲ Average energy output

Area of UK	Average wind speed (m/s)
southern England (mainly flat)	6
northern England (mainly hilly)	8
Lake District	12

E (i) According to the graph, what is the most efficient speed for a typical turbine to generate electricity? (ii) Use the table to decide what the average wind speed is where you live and find out how much electricity would be produced by a wind turbine in your area. (iii) Use this data to calculate how many turbines are needed to produce 2 MW where you live. (Level 8)

Assess your progress

7.2

1 What is the energy transfer that takes place when charging a mobile phone battery? (Level 4)

2 A TV transfers electrical energy as other forms of energy. What are these forms? (Level 5)

3 Food labels often describe the energy contained in a food in 'kilocalories (kcal)', which is an older unit for energy.
1 kcal = about 4 kilojoules (kJ). How many joules of energy would you gain by eating a 100 kilocalorie pear? (Level 6)

4 A hairdryer transfers 200 joules of electrical energy per second. It takes 5 minutes to dry your hair. How many joules of energy have been transferred? (Level 7)

5 A food mixer requires 300 joules of electrical energy and transfers 60% of the energy as unwanted energy.
  a How much energy, in joules, is dissipated?
  b What are the unwanted forms of energy? (Level 8)

7.3

1 A pupil claims that a 9 V battery is as dangerous as the mains supply (230 V). Is this true? Explain your answer. (Level 4)

2 A bulb and a buzzer are connected in series. The buzzer has a greater resistance. As current flows around the circuit, is more energy transferred to the buzzer or to the bulb? (Level 5)

3 Why can you buy a laptop that runs on a 10 V battery but not a 10 V battery-powered washing machine? (*Hint:* think about the forms of energy needed for each machine.) (Level 6)

4 A 6 V power pack is replaced by a 2 V power pack in a series circuit with two bulbs. How are the bulbs affected and why? (Level 7)

5 A circuit has two components in series. One has twice the resistance of the other. The voltage of the supply is 9 V. What is the voltage across each component? (Level 8)

7.4

1 How much energy does a 40 W bulb require to run for 10 minutes? (Level 4)
2 A manufacturer puts a washing machine onto rubber feet. How might this make the washing machine more efficient? (Level 5)
3 Today's washing powders are designed to wash clothes in cooler water. How does this affect the efficiency of a wash? (Level 6)
4 A kettle takes more power than a light bulb to operate. But in a single day, the energy transferred to a traditional light bulb may be more than the energy transferred to a kettle. Explain why. (Level 7)
5 Suppose the cost of electrical energy is 2 pence per 1000 kJ. How much does it cost to run a 3 kW heater for 10 hours? (Level 8)

7.5

1 Describe what you would need to do to boil a kettle without electricity. (Level 4)
2 Which of the methods of transferring energy into electrical energy in the spread do not use fuels? (Level 5)
3 It has been suggested that burning waste could be used to make steam. State an advantage and disadvantage of this idea. (Level 6)
4 Describe the energy transfers in a hydroelectric power station. (*Hint:* remember the water is stored in a reservoir high in the mountains before it is released to turn the turbine.) (Level 7)
5 It is impossible to create a machine that is 100% efficient. Why do you think all machines will dissipate some energy and in what form will this energy be dissipated? (Level 8)

7.6

1 Why is there a lot of interest in generating electricity from the wind? (Level 4)
2 Give a weighting from 0 to 10 for each opinion on page 124 for and against wind energy. (10 means you think the opinion is very important, 0 means you think it is not important.) Total the scores. Which opinions have the highest score – for or against? Does this agree with your point of view? (Level 5)
3 The government has decided that wind power is a good idea, but does not want to cover a lot of the countryside with them as local people often protest about the damage to views and tourism. Suggest two alternative ideas for the placement of turbines. (Level 6)
4 A typical home may use 0.002 MW of electricity. A typical power station produces 520 MW of energy. How many homes could this power station supply? (Level 7)
5 Using the tables and graphs in section 7.6 calculate how many homes a wind turbine could supply in:
a the Lake District
b southern England. (Level 8)

Focus on careers

Commercial pilots fly planes containing passengers or cargo around the world. They can be responsible for aircraft worth millions of pounds. Commercial pilots need to know how to take off and land a plane, how to navigate and what to do in an emergency. They can also specialise and take exams to fly helicopters or balloons and airships.

Architects design and oversee the construction of buildings. They need to understand the different ways that buildings can be constructed so they can work together with builders to produce what the client wants, on time and on budget. Architects also need to understand the regulations that control the construction of buildings as they often have to make important decisions that affect health and safety.

Energy, electricity and focus

Stephen is a **sound engineer**. He is involved in designing, operating and installing sound equipment. Sound engineers often work in recording studios with musicians where they use sound technology to record or mix sounds. They can also work on sound for TV programmes, films and video games, as well as live events such as shows and concerts.

Being a **chef**, like Donna, involves knowing how different ingredients will react when they are mixed together, as well as knowing what happens when you heat them in different ways. It is also important for her to know what combinations of food will taste good. She also needs to be able to measure ingredients accurately. Chefs have to pay very close attention to health and safety issues. They need to know how to keep their working environment clean and safe as well as how to prevent food becoming contaminated.

Pharmacists can work in hospitals, clinics and chemist shops. One of their jobs is to dispense medicine to people who give them a medical prescription from a doctor. They also tell people how to take the medicine and what might happen when they take it. Pharmacists can specialise in other areas of pharmacy such as drug information pharmacy, veterinary pharmacy or industrial pharmacy.

Chemical and material behaviour

As well as putting out fires, **firefighters** rescue people from burning buildings or from being trapped in cars after accidents. They are also involved in fire prevention. Firefighters need to have a good knowledge of how different materials burn as well as the best ways to put them out. Firefighters often work closely with the other emergency services such as ambulance crews or the police.

Dog trainers can work for private customers, vets or pet shelters. Some are involved in training police dogs, but others can train guide dogs for the blind. Dog trainers need to understand how dogs learn and how different dogs behave. They train dogs to understand hand signals or voice commands. They also teach the dogs' owners how to control their dogs.

Midwives, like Lucy, care for mothers before their babies are born. They help during the birth and care for the mothers and babies after the birth. Midwives are also involved in health education, including giving mothers information on what will happen during the birth and how to care for their babies after they are born. Most midwives work for the National Health Service but some work privately.

Organisms, behaviour and health

Horticulturalists can be involved in producing and growing plants, breeding new plants, or genetic engineering. Some specialise in trees – others specialise in floriculture, which is the production of flowers, or pomology, which is the production of fruit. Some horticulturalists are involved in crop production, including working out how to improve crop yield, quality and nutritional value and control disease and pest resistance.

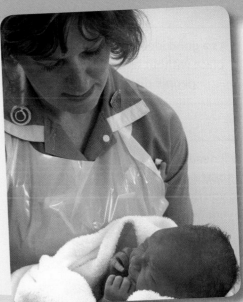

Environmental Health Officers, like Dan, mostly work for local authorities. His job involves investigating pollution and prosecuting people who break the law. He may visit homes to check out complaints about noise or rubbish, or he may visit cafes and shops to check they are hygienic. He may also visit factories to check if they are causing pollution.

Weather forecasters usually use computer models to predict what the weather will be like. An important part of their job is predicting when high winds, floods or fog might happen so people can be warned. Weather forecasters need to be able to choose the best model for a forecast by being able to recognise patterns, plus understand how models work and what problems they might have.

The environment, Earth and Universe

Seismologists study earthquakes and the effects of earthquakes, such as tsunamis. Seismologists also study the causes of earthquakes and try to predict the possibilities of an earthquake happening in a particular place at a particular time. Some field seismologists use controlled explosions to search for oil or gas. Other seismologists are involved in developing early warning systems for earthquakes so that people can be evacuated.

How to revise

We've got tests coming up soon.

How can we remember everything we've learned?

You will do your best in science tests if you revise before the test. Here are some tips and hints to help you.

Where to revise

It's a good idea to revise in a quiet place without television or other people disturbing you.

You will need a good source of light so you don't strain your eyes.

Make sure you can spread all your things out.

Get together everything you need such as books, notes, blank paper and pens and pencils.

How to revise

It doesn't matter how you revise – the most important thing is that you revise actively because this makes it easier to remember what you've learned. Revising actively means doing activities rather than just trying to read and remember stuff.

As well as remembering the key points in a topic, it is also important that you understand the processes that scientists carry out when they do science. This includes planning experiments, collecting data from observations and measurements, plus thinking about whether the data is accurate and reliable.

Coming up with theories to explain the data is very important. Scientists also have to think carefully about what impact their discoveries will have on people and the environment, and whether what they are doing is moral and ethical.

There are lots of ways you can revise actively depending on whether you learn best by looking at diagrams and pictures, listening or by doing activities, such as quizzes. You can read some suggestions below.

Read a topic. Close your book and write down as many key points as you can. Open the book and check what you've written. Go over the things you didn't remember. Repeat until you can remember everything in a topic.

Use mnemonics or rhymes to remember key points such as: 'Energy is conserved. Isn't that absurd?'

Record or video yourself or a friend talking about the key points in a topic and play it back often.

Make a key facts poster or a mind map for a topic and put it on the wall.

Do some question and answer sessions with a friend.

When to revise

Don't:

- leave all your revision until the night before the test and then try to cram it all in
- revise for hours without a break
- revise late at night when you are tired
- try to keep revising if you are tired or distracted and you are not taking anything in.

Do:

- leave yourself plenty of time before the test to revise
- revise regularly
- break up your revision. Revise for half an hour, have a break for ten minutes and then start again.

Revision timetables

It helps to break down topics into smaller sections and revise one section at a time. It can also help to plan your revision using a timetable. Make a list of all the topics you need to cover and then work out how much time you have before the exam to revise. Work out how you will divide the topics up between the days – try to cover every topic at least twice and preferably three times. Having a session where you go over the topics you have revised again can be helpful.

Suggested revision timetable		
Day	**Topic**	**Tick when done**
1	topic 1	
2	topic 2	
3	topic 3	
4	topic 1, 2, 3	
5	topic 4	

You could also have a revision timetable where you go over topic 1 after 24 hours, again after a week and then again after one month. You would do the same with the rest of the topics.

Before the test

▲ Get plenty of sleep the night before

▲ Try and do lots of exercise

▲ Drink lots of water. It keeps your brain hydrated and you will be more alert. Eating healthily is also important

SPEED DATING

Best Science Lesson Ever

Before you start

Your teacher will divide your class into two groups. One group will be the speed-daters and the other group will be the dates. You will be asked to provide an ID card with some interesting facts about yourself.

The speed-daters will be asked to learn a whole topic and come to the event with a list of relevant questions and answers. The dates will be asked to learn three topics in detail.

What to do

On the day of the event you will mingle with the other speed-daters and dates. You will have five minutes to introduce yourself and you can only mention interesting facts relating to the topic.

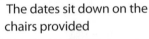

The dates sit down on the chairs provided

The speed-daters are given a score sheet and they choose who they want to talk to

The speed-daters have three minutes to question their dates

If you are a speed-dater, you need to assess your three dates according to the criteria on your score sheet. Rank your dates after you have suggested where they can improve their knowledge. Put your completed sheets on the speed-dating board.

BEEP-BEEP!

After three minutes the buzzer will sound and the speed-daters move on to their next dates

Rating the dates

You have now come to the end of your speed-dating experience. It is now time to evaluate.

A How was the speed-dating revision lesson different to your normal revision lesson?

B Which parts of the lesson would you change and why?

Speed Dating

Name:

- How do you rate your speed dating experst
- Your final rating must take into account knowledge and understanding of the subject

Date Name	Topic	Questions asked	Comments on K & U	Rank
1				
2				
3				

Rank criteria

	Has very good knowledge of topic. Has very good use of science language. Is able to label diagrams without using a text book.
	Has a good understanding of the topic. Can use some keywords correctly. Does need some help explaining some scientific ideas.
	Needs to revise more! Can only use basic scientific knowledge to explain scientific ideas.

C (i) Did you find the improvement targets useful? (ii) How would you use them to help improve your learning?

Voted a Best Lesson at Bartley Green School

What is How Science Works?

The *Go Science!* pupil books and activities often talk about 'How Science Works' but what exactly is this? How Science Works is not just about doing practical experiments – it is also about understanding how science affects your life and what sort of questions science can help you answer.

How Science Works has five main parts. Key Stage 3 covers each of these areas as well as the science content you learn. The five main parts are:

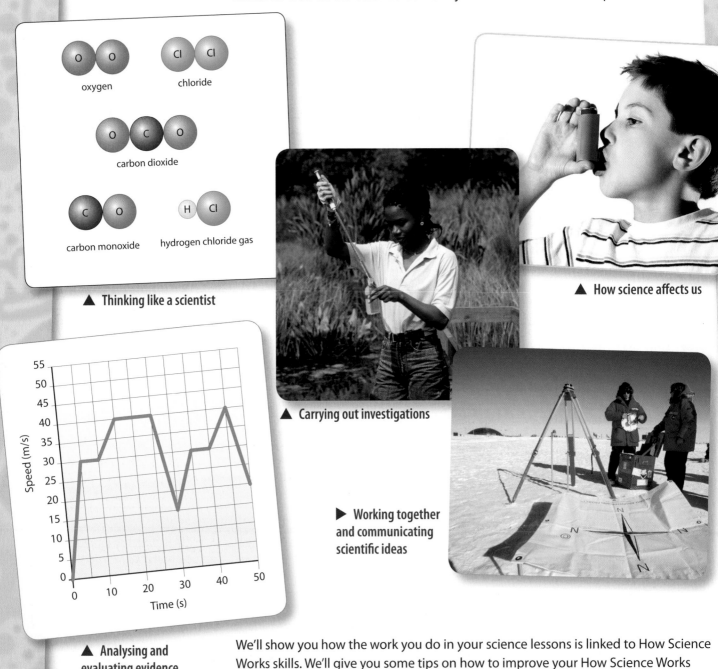

▲ Thinking like a scientist

▲ Carrying out investigations

▲ How science affects us

▶ Working together and communicating scientific ideas

▲ Analysing and evaluating evidence

We'll show you how the work you do in your science lessons is linked to How Science Works skills. We'll give you some tips on how to improve your How Science Works skills to boost your levels when you take tests.

The diagrams on the next pages show you how to move from one level to the next.

Skill 1: Thinking like a scientist

Scientists use models to explain the World around us. You do this when you talk about particles and when you made the pizza model of an animal cell in *Go Science! 1*. Sometimes you can improve the model – to turn the animal cell into a plant cell you could put the pizza into a cardboard box. The box would represent the plant cell wall.

Hot tip

To think like a scientist you need to be able to use scientific evidence. It is not enough to say: I think a larger volume of water will take longer to boil. You also need the evidence to back your statement up.

Level 4	Level 5	Level 6	Level 7	Level 8
I can describe a scientific idea using a simple model, e.g. drawing a force as an arrow. I can identify scientific evidence that is used to support an argument.	I can use a model to explain a scientific process, e.g. the water model to explain current in a circuit. I can say when scientists have used creative thinking when developing their ideas.	I can identify the strengths and weaknesses of a model. I can use evidence to support a scientific idea, e.g. pressure increases as temperature increases, supporting the particle model.	I can explain changes I have observed using a model, e.g. the particle model to explain a chemical reaction. I can explain how different bits of evidence support a scientific idea.	I can explain how new evidence causes a scientific idea to be changed. I can explain a process in detail using ideas and models from different areas of science.

Skill 2: How science affects us

Scientists make amazing discoveries – they've found things that really change the way you lead your life, such as electricity. But using scientific discoveries may bring problems as well as benefits, for example nuclear power does not produce carbon dioxide, which is good, but it does produce radioactive waste.

Hot tip

You need to be able to judge the positive as well as the negative outcomes of applying science to solve the World's problems.

Level 4	Level 5	Level 6	Level 7	Level 8
I can describe an application of a scientific idea, e.g. when things burn they need oxygen. Using a fire blanket cuts out the oxygen and the fire goes out.	I can describe an ethical issue coming from a scientific development, e.g. it is possible to choose the sex of your child. But should parents be allowed to do this?	I can describe how the uses of science or technology may be different in different societies.	I can list the moral, ethical, social arguments for and against a scientific development, e.g. genetic engineering.	I can evaluate ethical, moral or social arguments for or against a scientific development, e.g. the pros and cons of nuclear power.

Skill 3: Carrying out investigations

Hot tip

In investigations you need to keep some variables constant while changing the independent variable.

During Key Stage 3 you carry out several scientific investigations. Sometimes you plan the enquiry and carry out a risk assessment to make sure you work safely, and you may select the correct equipment to use. You then collect data, sometimes using precision instruments such as digital thermometers or electronic balances to get accurate results. In all these situations you are working like a scientist.

Level 4	Level 5	Level 6	Level 7	Level 8
I can make a series of observations and measurements, e.g. heating ice and measuring the temperature as it changes to water. I can follow instructions to reduce risks to myself.	I can repeat a series of measurements and observations. I can suggest ways to control risks to myself and others.	I can identify independent and dependent variables. I can recognise a risk and take action to control it.	I can identify key variables or ones that cannot easily be controlled. I know when to carry out a risk assessment.	I can choose a way of collecting data that produces precise and reliable results. I can control risk by consulting and adapting sources of information.

Skill 4: Analysing and evaluating evidence

Hot tip

Putting results into a table or a graph helps you identify a pattern more easily and make conclusions.

When you look at your results it may be obvious how you could improve the investigation or the 'repeatability' of the measurements you make. It is also important that you realise that your data alone may not be enough to prove a hypothesis. Sometimes different evidence is conflicting – you need to be able to explain why this might be so.

Level 4	Level 5	Level 6	Level 7	Level 8
I can identify a pattern in data and draw a conclusion from the data. I can suggest a way to improve the investigation.	I can identify inconsistencies in data and suggest why repeated measurements may be different. I can suggest ways to improve my method of working in an investigation.	I can suggest why the data or evidence I collect may be limited. I can recognise that evidence I collect may be limited and suggest why this might be so.	I can identify relationships between variables, e.g. the number of paperclips picked up by an electromagnet and the strength of the current. I can decide whether the data is sufficient to support my conclusion.	I can carry out a multi-step calculation. I can suggest a strategy to continue the investigation, e.g. how an investigation into the porosity of rocks could be continued, by looking at a wider range of rocks and/or examining rock slides under a microscope.

Skill 5: Working together and communicating scientific ideas

In *Go Science!* you come across lots of examples of teams of scientists working together to solve problems. When scientists work together they need to be able to explain their findings to each other. In the same way, when you produce reports and tables and graphs of your data, you need to use scientific language and present your findings in a way that is clear to others.

Hot tip

When you research on the Internet, you need to find evidence from a reliable source with scientific data that can be relied upon.

Level 4	Level 5	Level 6	Level 7	Level 8
I can choose an appropriate way to present scientific data. I can communicate a scientific idea using scientific language.	I can list some scientific breakthroughs that needed teams of scientists, e.g. flat screen televisions. I can decide on when to use line graphs to present scientific data.	I can give an example of an advance in scientific knowledge made by a multidisciplinary team, e.g. biologists and chemists working to produce new vaccines. I can choose a way to communicate data which is relevant to the audience.	I can explain how scientists from different backgrounds work together on a scientific development, e.g. chemists design a new drug and biologists test the effects on living tissue. I can use symbols and flow diagrams to communicate scientific information.	I can explain how scientists with different skills work together to find a solution to a multidisciplinary problem, e.g. satellites for weather forecasting. I can evaluate evidence from different sources, explaining limitations or bias.

This is a Level 4 question. You need to read the whole question before you start answering. Try to imagine doing the investigation yourself:

I was doing an investigation into the best type of electric kettle to buy. I wanted to find out whether some makes were quicker to heat up than others and whether some makes were quieter than others.

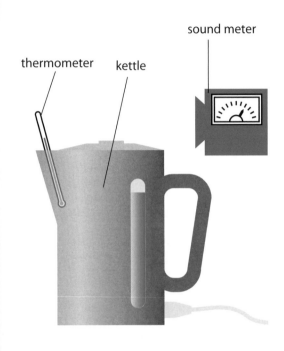

thermometer   kettle   sound meter

Q1 I measured the temperature of water in an electric kettle from when I turned it on until after the thermostat turned it off. I also measured the sound it made. I wanted to find out at what temperature the kettle made most sound.

These are my results:

Time (seconds)	Temperature (°C)	Sound (dB)
0	22	51
30	25	51
60	44	75
90	61	84
120	78	86
150	95	78
180	99	51
210	96	54
240	94	52

a How many minutes did the experiment take? (1 mark)

Change seconds to minutes. You need to calculate how many lots of 60 there are in the time column – this is called 'interpreting numbers' and is a Level 4 skill.

b What was the independent variable in this experiment? (1 mark)

The independent variable is the thing you decide to change when doing the experiment. In this case the experimenter decided to take a measurement every 30 seconds so time is the independent variable. A clue is that the independent variable is usually the first column in a table of data.

c What was the loudest sound recorded in the table? (1 mark)

Clue – find the sound column and move your pen down the list till it gets to the biggest number then stop if the numbers start to get smaller again. Check there are no larger numbers lower down in the column and then write down the number next to your pen as the answer. This is the same sort of skill as in part a.

d Estimate from the results table the number of seconds taken for the water to reach 100 °C. (1 mark)

Find the temperature that is closest to 100 – which is 99. In this case the water boiled after 180 seconds but before 210 seconds. You will get a mark for any number between 180 and 210. A good answer would be closer to 180 than 210, around 185. Because the question says estimate, you know that there is a range of acceptable answers.

e Describe the pattern for the change in temperature. (1 mark)

Describing patterns wants you to say in words the story told by the numbers. Saying 'the temperature changes from 22 to 94' would be a poor answer. Saying 'the temperature increased up to a maximum and then fell slightly' would be a better answer. It is also a good answer to say 'the temperature rose for 180 seconds before cooling slightly' – so there is more than one way of answering. You will get a mark if you can show that you understand what the numbers mean.

f Describe the pattern for the change in sound. (1 mark)

Do the same for this question as for part e. The answer for sound is not the same as the answer for temperature because here the sound went up quickly and then came down quickly to the starting point.

g At what temperature did the kettle make the most sound? (1 mark)

Match the highest number in the sound column to the temperature on the same row. This is more difficult to get right than part c but it is still a Level 4 question. Only one number – 78 – will get you the mark.

h The experiment was to find out at what temperature the kettle made most sound. How could the experiment be improved to make the answer more accurate? (1 mark)

You can get a mark for writing one of several different right answers for this question. Possible answers include: 'do the experiment in a soundproof environment to make sure only the sound from the kettle was recorded' and 'do a trial experiment first to make sure that the sensors were placed in a position that measured the maximum change in temperature and sound'.

You could also explain how the experiment could have been modified to check the reliability of the data recorded. Only give one answer but make sure you have explained why your answer would make the experiment more accurate. Do not say the instruments are faulty or the experimenter lacked skill.

Choose answers that show you understand how the experiment was set up and why the design of the experiment needs to be improved. This is the only part of the question that is Level 5. For level 5 you need to be able to say 'why' as well as 'what'.

Practice question 2

This is a Level 5 question. A Level 6 question would ask you to choose the scale for the graph and also ask you to explain the results rather than to describe the results. Unless you know a lot about bicycle technology and the cyclists involved it would be very difficult to explain the results in this investigation.

World record time (min-sec)	Date	Venue	Team
4-24.91	1976	Milan	Italy
4-23.07	1979	Zurich	Switzerland
4-16.62	1980	Moscow	USSR
4-14.26	1984	Moscow	USSR
4-12.83	1986	Moscow	USSR
4-10.08	1991	Stuttgart	Germany
4-03.84	1993	Hamar	Australia
4-00.96	1996	Manchester	Italy
3-59.71	2000	Sydney	Germany
3-59.58	2002	Manchester	Australia
3-57.28	2003	Stuttgart	Australia
3-56.61	2004	Athens	Australia
3-56.32	2008	Manchester	Great Britain

Q2 The team pursuit is a track cycling event involving two teams of four cyclists racing for 4000 m.

Since 1976 the World record time for this event has improved.

Here are some data on the left on team pursuit World records.

Your task is to analyse the data using a graph.

a The data have been put into a different format in a new table on the right. Complete the table. (1 mark)

You must fill in all five boxes, making sure you copy the numbers correctly into each box. When you have answered the question look back at the first table to make sure your answers are correct. This is a Level 5 question because the numbers you are working with are complex and have decimal points.

Time (date)	World record time (seconds)
1976	264.91
1979	263.07
1980	256.62
1984	254.26
1986	252.83
1991	250.08
1993	243.84
1996	240.96
2000	
2002	
2003	
2004	
2008	

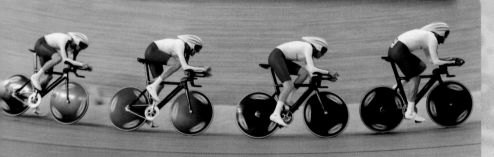

b Draw a graph of World record time against year on the axes below. (2 marks)

You must plot the points correctly and draw a line between them to get both marks. In this case it is not possible to plot each point accurately to two decimal places so you can round them up or down to the nearest whole number. Mark each point with a cross and not a blob.

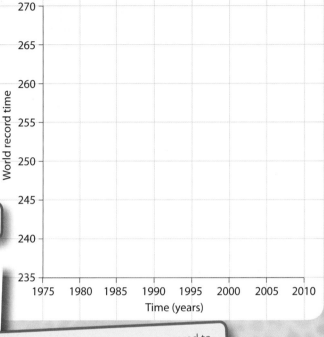

c In which year was the greatest improvement in the World record? (1 mark)

1993 is the only answer allowed.

d What evidence is there that the greatest improvements happen in Olympic Games years? (1976, 1980, 1984, 1988, 1992, 1996, 200, 2004) (1 mark)

Mark on your graph where each of the Games years appeared to help you identify any evidence that the greatest improvements happen in Olympic Games years.

e What evidence is there that the greatest improvements happen outside the Olympic Games years? (1 mark)

Compare improvements made in Olympic years with improvements made in other years. Identify any year which was not an Olympic year when a big improvement was made.

f What additional evidence should be collected to confirm the theory that team pursuit world records improve most in Olympic Games years? (1 mark)

Collect information from a greater range of years. In your answer say that you need to compare record times in Olympic years with records set in other years for dates before 1976.

g What is your answer to the question: 'Do World records improve a little bit each year or do they make big jumps?' (1 mark)

There is not enough evidence to say one way or the other so you must explain that there is evidence for both. You do not need to explain what further work you would do to find out the answer.

Project 1 A way of life

Learn about:

- a way to measure your fitness
- how to have a healthy lifestyle
- how other nations live a healthy life

▲ Are vitamin supplements part of a healthy lifestyle?

Healthy living is not just about eating a balanced diet. It's also about how you look after your body, how you exercise and how you provide your body with the nutrients it needs.

Our Government often gives advice on how to live healthily. Why? What part does science play in this? Do all countries have the same commitment to improving the health of their nation?

You are going to be researching and investigating healthy living. Once you have gathered your information you will need to present your findings. There are many ways that you can present data: either as a written report, a presentation to your class, a video report or a poster.

How fit are you?

You have already seen that one way of measuring fitness is to use pulse rate. When sitting, your pulse rate is slow and steady – this is your **resting rate**. During exercise your pulse rate increases. After exercise, as your body recovers your pulse rate returns to its resting rate. The time taken to do this is called the **recovery rate**. The quicker this time, the fitter you are.

▲ How long can you hold a stool out for? This is a test of stamina!

Activity 1

Carry out an investigation to discover how fit you are compared to other people in your class. Each person in the class needs to do the same exercise for the same amount of time. Once completed the results can be compiled in a table and analysed to find fitness range. Research different exercise regimes and assess their benefits.

Why do we sleep?

An important part of healthy living is sleep. While you are asleep your body has the chance to rest. Dreaming is your body's way of processing all the day's events. Lack of sleep affects your brain's ability to function correctly. Sleep patterns vary according to age with a teenager needing about 10 hours per night. Sleep needs also vary according to the individual – Napoleon only needed 4 hours of sleep each night!

Activity 2

Conduct a survey to discover how many hours of sleep people in your class get each night. What do they do before they go to bed? Does this affect their ability to fall asleep?

Interesting fact

Dolphins and ducks keep half of their brains awake while the other half sleeps so they can always be on the watch for predators.

Are vitamin supplements necessary?

Eating five portions of fruit and vegetables each day should provide you with enough vitamins to keep you healthy. So why take vitamin supplements? Some people think that taking extra vitamin C will stop you catching a cold. There have even been claims that taking extra vitamins can prevent or cure illnesses such as heart disease and cancer. But is this true? Vitamin C is known to help symptoms of colds but can't actually prevent you from catching one. Your body will only absorb the vitamins it needs and will excrete the rest.

Activity 3

Research the range of vitamin supplements you can buy, how much they cost and their health benefits. Are there any particular times in life when taking vitamin supplements would be beneficial? Produce a report to show your findings.

Fighting the obesity war

The number of people classed as obese in the UK is rising rapidly, with nearly a quarter of all adults now classed as clinically obese. Experts are warning of an **obesity** epidemic and are blaming poor diets and lack of exercise. A person is classed as obese when there is a significant amount of fat on their body and it has an impact on their health.

Activity 4

Research two countries – one Western country and one from the developing world – and their attitudes towards healthy living. Include information on diet, exercise and government response to the health of the nation. How do these countries compare to the UK? Are we a healthy country?

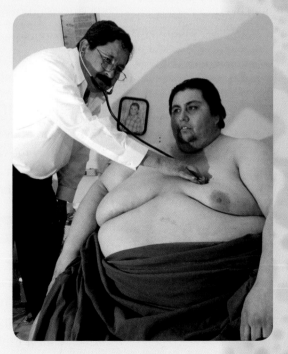

▲ A poor diet and lack of exercise can have a devastating effect on the human body

Keywords
obesity, recovery rate, resting rate

Project 2 | Whatever the weather

Learn about:

- recording the weather
- the global impact of severe weather
- how scientists track weather

▲ Hurricanes look beautiful from above, but can cause terrible devastation below

Interesting fact

In October 1987 the UK had the worst storm since the 1700s, costing 18 lives and £1 billion to clear up. **Meteorologists** did not predict the storm so everyone was caught unawares.

Weather can be dangerous. Storms, heatwaves and floods can cause devastation and death, so the weather is constantly monitored to warn people and minimise risk.

Weather is used to describe the conditions in the atmosphere and air around you and can include temperature, wind speed and direction, precipitation, sunshine and clouds.

In this project you are going to make a weather station, collect data, research different weather events and present your work. You may wish to present your work as a report, a PowerPoint presentation, a video diary or as a weather forecaster on a TV show.

Tracking and recording weather data

Everybody likes to know what the weather has in store for them, so **meteorologists** study the weather and forecast what you can expect. They look at satellite pictures of cloud formations, study data on temperature and wind and use computer-generated maps to track weather patterns to predict what the weather will do.

Activity 1

Use the BBC weather site to predict the maximum and minimum temperatures for your location over the next 5 days. Then measure the actual temperatures using either a maximum–minimum thermometer or a datalogger based near to your classroom. You can record the information in a table like the one below.

Day/date	Predicted maximum temperature (°C)	Predicted minimum temperature (°C)	Measured maximum temperature (°C)	Measured minimum temperature (°C)

Severe weather

Severe weather can happen anytime and anywhere. In August 2004 Boscastle in Cornwall was hit by a heavy storm that resulted in major flooding. In August 2005 Hurricane Katrina passed over New Orleans in America and left 80% of the city under water. Catastrophic weather events such as these have a major impact on people when they lose their families, homes and belongings. They also have a countrywide and global impact, with repairing and rebuilding areas having a major economic effect.

Activity 2

Part 1 – Make a rainfall gauge and see how much precipitation your area experiences every day for a week. Record your findings in a table.
Part 2 – Research a recent flood. Include in your findings the date the flood happened, the weather prior to the flood, whether meteorologists had predicted the flood, how bad the flood was and the damage that was caused, plus any other interesting facts.

▲ The aftermath of the Boscastle flood

The history of weather

A **barometer** measures air pressure. High air pressure usually means fine weather and low pressure indicates that storms are more likely. Barometers were one of the first ways of predicting weather and mapping weather patterns. They can produce quite accurate predictions when used with wind measurements.

Official weather records start from 1914 but unofficial records start from the seventeenth century. Meteorologists use these records to compare the weather we have today with that of the past and to see if climates really are changing due to human impact.

Activity 3

Make a barometer and a wind-speed meter. Record the results for a week. When pressure is high is the weather fine? What is the weather like when wind speeds are high? Research weather records and see if you can find any data that shows how climate has changed over the last 100 years.

▲ It takes a long time for an area to recover from a major weather disaster

Early warning systems

Scientists are continually developing new technology to help forecast weather events as early as possible. One system combines geographical information with descriptive information about what the weather is like. This enables scientists to analyse trends and patterns so predictions can be made. Another system uses a numerical model to predict weather patterns. These, along with satellite imagery and radar technology, can provide important early warnings for severe weather systems before they hit an area.

Activity 4

Research how far in advance we get our weather forecasts at the moment. How do meteorologists predict what our weather will be like?

Keywords
barometer, meteorologist

Glossary

acceleration An increase in speed.

acid rain Rain polluted by acidic gases dissolved in it. It has a pH below 6.

addicted When someone develops a mental or physical dependency on a drug they are said to be addicted.

adsorbed When one material is stuck on to, bonds to or forms a chemical attachment to the surface of another material.

aerobic respiration A form of respiration that requires oxygen to release the chemical energy in glucose for use by the cell.

air resistance The frictional force between air particles and an object moving through them.

anaerobic respiration A form of respiration that does not require oxygen to release the chemical energy in glucose for use by the cell.

animal testing The use of animals for scientific experimentation, especially for testing drugs.

antagonistic pair A pair of muscles that pull a bone in opposite directions.

archaeologist A scientist who studies the material remains of past human life and activities.

arthritis A disease that causes inflammation of joints which is painful and affects mobility.

artificial satellite A device launched into space which orbits a planet.

asexual reproduction The process by which new organisms are produced from one parent only.

asteroid A rock, smaller than a planet, that moves freely through Space. There are a lot of asteroids in orbit around the Sun.

asthma A respiratory disease which causes inflammation of the bronchial tubes.

bacteriologist A scientist who studies bacteria and other microorganisms.

balanced equation A symbol equation for a reaction in which the number of atoms of each element is the same on the right and the left.

ball and socket joint A type of joint within the body that gives a wide range of movement.

barometer An instrument used to measure air pressure which is especially helpful in weather forecasting.

base A substance that neutralises an acid but is not soluble in water.

bicep A muscle in the upper arm that works with the tricep and moves the elbow.

binge drinking Drinking large quantities of alcohol in a short space of time.

biodegradable Can be broken down in the environment.

biodiversity The number of different species of living things.

biofuel A fuel produced from plant sources.

biogas digester Equipment used for producing a supply of methane gas from food, animal or plant waste.

birth mother The animal into which the fertilised egg is implanted. The egg will develop in the uterus of this animal and she will give birth to it. She is also known as a surrogate mother.

boiler The part of a power station where water is heated.

bone A rigid tissue that forms part of the skeleton.

bronchitis An infection of the bronchial tubes.

carbon cycle A model of how carbon enters, is used by and is released from plants, animals, fuels and other materials.

carbon neutral A process which uses up as much carbon dioxide as it produces.

centre of mass The point on an object at which gravity acts.

chemical formula Chemical symbol used to show the atoms in a substance.

chromatography A technique used to separate components in a mixture according to their solubility.

cilia Small hairs found on cells that line the trachea which help trap debris.

Class A The most dangerous type of drugs in drug classification.

Class B Drugs that are more dangerous than Class C drugs, but less dangerous than Class A drugs.

Class C The least dangerous types of drugs in drug classification.

climate change The change in general weather patterns thought to be caused by warming of the Earth.

clinical trial The use of humans to test for effects, both wanted and unwanted, of a substance.

clone An exact genetic copy of an organism.

collaboration Working together to help each other.

communication satellite A satellite that is used for telecommunications.

compost heap A household collection of plant and food waste which usually becomes compost for the garden.

compressed Squeezed into less space.

condensation Gas turning to a liquid as it cools.

condenser The apparatus used in a laboratory to cool a gas so that it turns into a liquid.

conjoined twins Twins who are joined by certain organs or body parts. These twins are formed when a fertilised egg splits, as it does to form identical twins, but the split is incomplete so that the individuals are joined.

conservation of matter The fact that matter is not made or destroyed during a chemical reaction.

control A sample set up in an experiment to allow comparison.

correlation A link between two variables.

crude oil A mixture of hydrocarbons made over millions of years from the remains of marine animals.

cryogenics The study of chemicals and processes at very cold temperatures.

current Current flows around a circuit carrying energy from the supply to the components.

cylinder A part of a hydraulic machine. The plunger moves along it.

deceleration A decrease in speed.

desirable feature A feature which has advantages for the organism or for the scientist, farmer or gardener breeding it.

diaphragm The sheet of muscle below the lungs.

disinfection The process of killing bacteria.

displacement reaction The replacement of one element in a compound by another element.

distance–time graph A graph that shows how far an object has moved in a certain time.

distillation A method used to separate a mixture of liquids with different boiling points by evaporation and condensation.

donor mother The animal that provides the cell nucleus which is placed in an egg cell and implanted into the birth mother.

double-blind trial A trial in which the subjects and the scientists do not know if they are being given a drug or a placebo.

drag The frictional force between gas or liquid particles and an object moving through them.

drug A chemical that affects the way your body works.

efficiency rating A code which indicates the relative energy efficiency of a machine.

electrolysis Decomposition of a compound into its elements by the passage of electricity.

electromagnet A magnet that can be switched on and off using electricity.

elliptical orbit Planets orbiting a star move around a path that is elliptical in shape. An ellipse looks like a squashed circle.

endorphins 'Feel good' hormones that are released into your body when you exercise.

energy conservation The idea that energy cannot be created or destroyed. The amount of energy after an energy transfer is equal to the amount of energy before it took place.

energy dissipation The transfer of energy from a device as unwanted forms, such as when energy is transferred as heat where there is friction between moving parts.

energy efficiency The percentage of energy supplied to a device that is transferred as useful forms.

escape velocity The minimum speed at which a spacecraft without rockets must leave a planet's surface to avoid being pulled back to the surface by gravity.

European Energy Label A label attached to all new appliances sold in Europe to inform customers of the appliance's energy efficiency.

evaporation Liquid turning to a vapour as it warms.

exert When you exert pressure on something, you apply a force on it.

exothermic A term describing a reaction that gives out heat energy.

exploration satellite A satellite that takes photos and measurements of planet surfaces to help map and identify what's there.

fitness A measure of how well your heart and lungs deliver oxygen to the cells around your body.

forensic science The use of science to aid the operation of the legal system.

fossil-fuel power station A power station that uses fossil fuels to heat water.

fractional distillation A type of distillation used to separate a mixture of many liquids with similar boiling points.

fractionating column Glass column used to help separate liquids of similar boiling points during fractional distillation.

fractionating tower Equipment used in an oil refinery to separate crude oil into useful products.

G This number is needed in Newton's equation for gravitational attraction.

galaxy A cluster of billions of stars that swirl around a centre.

galvanising The process of coating a metal with a layer of zinc.

gene Small length of genetic material.

generator The part of a power station that transfers kinetic energy as electrical energy.

genetic counsellor A scientist with a knowledge of genes who can advise individuals with a family history of genetic disease.

genetic engineering The process of changing the genes which an organism naturally carries. Genes might be removed and replaced with alternative genes from the same or a different species.

genetic material The complex chemicals present in the nucleus of cells which are passed on from parents to offspring and which give organisms their features.

genetically modified (GM) A plant or animal which has had its genes altered.

geneticist A scientist with a knowledge of genes and how they act to produce an organism's features.

geocentric A model of the Solar System with the Earth at the centre.

geophysicist A scientist who studies the physics of the Earth and its environment.

global warming The increase in the average global temperature.

gradient The slope of a line on a graph.

gravimeter A device that measures the force of gravitational attraction at a location.

gravity map A map that shows how the pulling force of gravitational attraction on a 1 kg mass varies across an area.

gravity survey A survey in which the aim is to measure the forces of gravitational attraction in a particular area.

greenhouse gas A gas, such as carbon dioxide, that stops heat energy escaping from the Earth.

heliocentric A model of the Solar System with the Sun at the centre.

hinge joint A type of joint within the body that gives a backwards and forwards movement.

hormone A chemical produced by glands in the body that has a specific effect on particular organs.

hydraulic machine A machine that works by transferring pressure through a liquid.

hydraulics A system that uses the pressure of a liquid to transfer a force.

hydrocarbon A compound made of hydrogen and carbon atoms only.

hydroelectric power station A power station that uses falling water to turn a turbine.

identical twins Two individuals with the same genetic make-up formed when a fertilised egg splits and goes on to produce two individuals rather than one.

illegal drugs Substances that governments have decided are potentially very harmful and are illegal to possess.

immune system The body's natural defence against infection.

incineration Burning waste to destroy it.

joule (J) The unit of energy.

kilojoule (kJ) 1000 joules.

kilowatt (kW) 1000 watts.

landfill site Where household waste is dumped after its collection by dustbin lorries.

lever A simple machine that can increase the turning effect of a force.

malaria A disease caused by a tiny, single-celled organism (parasite) which lives in the blood. It is injected into the blood stream when an infected mosquito bites an individual.

maximum speed The greatest speed at which an object can travel.

medical drugs Substances that are used to prevent, treat or cure diseases or illnesses. The sale of medical drugs is closely controlled.

metal hydroxide A compound containing metal, oxygen and hydrogen atoms.

metal oxide A compound containing metal and oxygen atoms.

meteorologist A scientist who studies and forecasts weather.

methane A hydrocarbon compound with the formula CH_4.

moment The turning effect of a force.

muscle fatigue This is caused by a build up of lactic acid in the muscles. It happens during exercise when the blood cannot supply the muscles with enough oxygen.

nature An individual's genetic inheritance. The genes that an individual has influence its features and characteristics.

navigation satellite A satellite that sends data to cars, boats and planes to help them calculate their position.

nuclear power station A power station that uses uranium to heat water and generate electricity.

nurture An individual's upbringing, experience and learning. These factors influence the features and characteristics of an individual.

nutrients Chemical substances required by all living things for healthy growth and development.

obesity An excess of body fat. Obesity can cause serious health problems.

observation satellite A satellite that is used to monitor the Earth and atmosphere such as a weather satellite.

oceanographer A scientist who studies physical, chemical and biological aspects of the oceans.

oil refinery Industrial plant where crude oil is separated into useful products.

orbit The path along which moons and satellites move around a planet, or the paths along which planets move around a star.

ore A rock that contains a metal or metal compound that can be usefully extracted.

organic matter Natural material such as plants and animals, that are living or have once been living or part of a living thing.

osteoarthritis A condition in which the protective covering of cartilage on the joints is worn away, leading to pain when bones rub together.

ovum Female sex cell which is also called an egg cell.

ozone A gas with the chemical formula O_3, containing three oxygen atoms bonded together. It is naturally present high in the atmosphere.

passive smoking Secondary inhalation of smoke.

perpetual motion machine A machine that once started will never stop.

personality The way in which an individual reacts, thinks and behaves.

photosynthesis The process by which plants use water and carbon dioxide to form glucose and oxygen using sunlight energy. They carry this out in their leaves using the green pigment chlorophyll.

physiotherapy The treatment and prevention of mobility problems through exercise.

piston The part of a hydraulic machine that moves along a cylinder.

pivot A point around which something turns.

placebo A 'dummy' drug that contains no medicine. These are included in drug trials to ensure a patient's response to a test is due to the drug itself.

pneumatic An object that contains gas under pressure.

pollen grain The male sex cell in plants.

pollen tube The tube that grows from a pollen grain down through the stigma and style into the ovary.

pollination The transfer of pollen from an anther to a stigma.

pollutant A harmful or unwanted chemical.

positive correlation A term used to explain a definite link between variables.

potential difference Another name for voltage.

power The rate at which an appliance draws energy from a supply.

power station A place where energy is transferred as electrical energy.

precipitation Any water that falls from the sky to the Earth. It can be in the form of rain, snow, sleet, drizzle or fog.

pressure The effect of a force spread over an area.

principle of moments In a balanced system, the clockwise moments equal the anticlockwise moments.

psychologist A scientist who studies the ways in which individuals learn and behave. Psychologists are interested in how behaviours are established.

pulse rate The speed at which your heart beats.

radioactive An element or object that emits nuclear energy.

reactive A substance which will undergo chemical reactions is said to be reactive.

reactivity series A list of metals in order of their reactivity.

reagent A chemical used in analysis or the production of other chemicals.

recovery rate The time taken for your pulse to return to resting rate after exercise.

recreational drugs Substances that have an effect on the body. It is not illegal to be in possession of these but they are addictive and can cause ill health.

recycle Use a material to make something else.

release angle The angle that an object, such as a javelin, is released at.

resistance The components in a circuit resist the flow of current. As the current flows through a high-resistance component, it transfers more energy than when it flows through a low-resistance component.

resting rate How fast the heart beats without exercise or stimulation.

runner A piece that grows from a plant and develops into a new plant where it touches the soil.

rust Hydrated iron oxide formed when iron reacts with oxygen and water.

sacrificial corrosion A more reactive metal corroding in place of a less reactive one.

salt A compound that is formed when an acid reacts with a metal or metal compound.

Sankey diagram A Sankey diagram represents the flow of energy through a system.

selective breeding To produce an animal or plant with desirable features by mating or crossing individuals which have the features so that they appear in future generations.

series circuit If there is only one route around the circuit, then this is a series circuit

settlement tank Where water is held to allow gravity to cause small particles to fall to the bottom.

sewage Waste water from drains.

sewage works Where waste water is filtered and disinfected.

sexual reproduction Producing a new organism by combining a male cell and a female cell from two parents.

sickle cell anaemia A disease produced by a gene which causes the oxygen-carrying red blood pigment, haemoglobin, to be abnormal. It cannot carry as much oxygen as normal haemoglobin and this causes anaemia. The abnormal haemoglobin changes the shape of the red cells so that they become sickle shaped and block blood vessels and organs, causing pain and damage.

side effect A secondary, unwanted effect of a drug.

skeleton The 206 bones of the human body form this structure to maintain the body's shape.

smog Fog polluted with smoke and gases.

solar panel A panel that transfers light energy as heat or electrical energy.

solubility The mass of a solute that dissolves in a fixed volume of solvent.

solvent Liquid into which a solute is dissolved to make a solution.

specialised cells A cell that is adapted to carry out a particular function is specialised.

speed–time graph A graph that shows how the speed of an object changes during a journey.

sports psychologist A scientist who studies an athlete's behaviour and emotions to help improve their performance.

sustainable Available for use in the future.

symbol equation An equation that uses chemical symbols to show what is happening during a chemical reaction.

take-off angle The angle at which a long jumper takes off.

take-off speed The speed at which a long jumper takes off.

thalidomide A drug that was given to pregnant women in the 1950s to prevent morning sickness, but resulted in babies with deformed limbs.

thermite reaction Exothermic displacement reaction between aluminium and iron oxide that produces molten iron.

trachea The tube that leads from the throat to the lungs (windpipe).

transgenic An organism which has been given genes from a different species.

transmit To pass from one place to another.

transpiration The process by which plants lose water from their leaves.

tricep A muscle in the upper arm that works with the bicep and moves the elbow.

turbine The part of a power station that steam or water causes to rotate. It is used to rotate the generator.

turning effect The effect of a force that allows an object to rotate around a pivot.

ultraviolet (UV) light High energy light beyond the violet end of the spectrum. It cannot be seen by the naked eye.

unreactive A substance which will not react with other substances is said to be unreactive.

variation The differences between two living things or between members of a species.

ventilation The movement of air in and out of the lungs.

voltage The voltage indicates the difference in electrical energy between two parts of a circuit. Voltage is also called potential difference.

water cycle A model of how water moves between the atmosphere, the land and the sea.

water pressure The pressure caused by the weight of water.

water treatment works Where water from reservoirs, rivers and other sources is treated to make it fit to drink.

watt (W) Unit of power. One watt is one joule per second.

wind farm A group of wind turbines.

withdrawal symptom Uncomfortable physical or mental change that happens when the body is deprived of a drug.

Index